THE CONNERYS

The making of a Waterford legend

Published in Ireland by
Geography Publications,
Kennington Road,
Templeogue, Dublin 6W

ISBN 0 906602 24 6

Cover design by Bernadette Kiely
Typesetting by Phototype-Set Ltd., Dublin
Printed by Colour Books, Dublin

Contents

DO MO MHUINTIR

Preface

In the opinion of Biddy Connery, who was an old woman in the 1920s, her relatives, the Connerys, were the greatest men that ever lived. She was one of the last of an Irish-speaking generation that remembered the three brothers and their exploits in the Waterford of the 1830s. This work began as an attempt to discover why she should make such a claim.

The story of Patrick, James and John Connery is one of epic confrontation with the magistracy, police and courts. By the time they had lost their unequal struggle with the authorities they had become potent symbols of agrarian violence and the factions. It was the manner in which the Connerys articulated, personalised and made explicit the whole tradition of agrarian dissent that translates an extraordinary story in a local context to an original contribution to Irish historiography of the 1830s.

However, that is not all, for the Connerys were sent as convicts to New South Wales. They never achieved an antipodean prominence to match that which they enjoyed at home, but their lives were not without incident. By recalling their time, both as convicts and freemen, that great enforced diaspora to the Australian continent, beginning with the *Queen* in 1791 and ending with the *Hougoumont* in 1868 is illuminated.

This is the story of the Connerys, covering eighty years of the nineteenth century and embracing the histories of both Ireland and New South Wales.

Acknowledgements

I am deeply indebted to Dr. John B. O'Brien for his expert advice, assistance and good humour over many years and not least for his work in the promotion of the study of Australian history in the South of Ireland. My special thanks to Professor John A. Murphy and Professor John Molony for their comments and suggestions.

I wish to thank the staff of the British Library; the Cork Archives Council; the Cork City Library; the Library of the Royal College of Surgeons; the National Library of Ireland; the Public Records Office of Ireland; the Public Records Office at Kew; Kensington Public Library; the National Maritime Museum at Greenwich; the Registry of Deeds; the Library of the Royal Irish Academy; the State Papers Office; the Waterford City Library; the Waterford County Library; the Library of University College Cork; the Library and the Department of Irish Folklore, University College Dublin for their attention and courtesy.

I am grateful to Very Reverend Dean Mayes of Lismore (now retired); Mr. Thomas Corcoran (grandson of Tomás Ó Corcoráin), Bohadoon, Dungarvan; Mr. John Kelly, Currabaha, Dungarvan; Most Reverend John Magee, Bishop of Cloyne; Reverend Fr. Denis Buckley, C.C., Mallow; the late Baron Brian de Breffny of Castletown, Carrick-on-Suir; Dr. David J. Burdon, Buttevant; Reverend Fr. Michael A. Cogan, P.P., Butttevant; Lord Heytesbury, Dorset; Reverend D.B.M. Warren, Stradbally, for their time and assistance. I must also thank all those involved in the preparation and publication of this book.

I wish to thank the Australian Embassy in Dublin, the Department of Immigration and Ethnic Affairs and my own employers, the Department of Social Welfare, for allowing me a year in New South Wales. I also wish to thank the staff of the Archives Office of New South Wales; the Mitchell Library, Sydney; the State Library of New South Wales; the Registry of Births, Deaths and Marriages, New South Wales; the Common Law Division of the Supreme Court of New South Wales; the Land Registry, Sydney; the Ferguson Memorial Library, Sydney; the Library of the Royal Australasian College of Physicians; the Waverley Municipal Library at Bondi; the State Library of South Australia; the State Library of Tasmania and Yass Library for their attention and courtesy.

I am much obliged to the descendants of the Connerys in New South Wales, in particular Ms. Carole Dick of Mona Vale, for allowing me to use her own research and for giving me the benefit of her own ideas; to Ms. Jacinta Connery of Erskineville for permission to reproduce the photograph of James Connery and for her help with the research. Thanks are also due to Ms. Rose Hodge of Gosford; Mr. Bruce Hodge of Orange;

Mr. Robert James Connery of Stokers Siding and Mr. John Connery of Maclean. I am also indebted to Dr. Marian and Mr. Eugene Sheehan of Bondi; Mr. James Sheehan and family of Cabramatta; the late Arnold Kearns of St. Mary's Cathedral and Leanne E. May of Adelaide.

I am further obliged to my cousins the late Mrs. Peggy Browne and Mr. Daniel Kiely for their enthusiasm and to the artist, Bernadette Kiely, for permission to use the illustration which appears on the cover. I must also mention my aunt, Sr. M. Rita Kiely, O.S.U., of Brentwood, Essex, who gave me great encouragement but unfortunately died before the book was completed. Finally I am deeply grateful to my parents Daniel and Alice; sisters Rita and Ann; brothers Patrick, Joseph and Dónal for all their help.

Táim buíoch do Ollscoil na hÉireann agus do Bord na Gaeilge a thug an cúnamh chun an leabhar seo a fhoilsiú.

Abbreviations

A.D.B.	Australian Dictionary of Biography
A.O.N.S.W.	Archives Office of New South Wales
C.A.	Colonial Architect
C.C.	Catholic Curate
C.S.I.L.	Colonial Secretary In-Letters
C.S.O.R.P.	Chief Secretary's Office Registered Papers
H.C.	House of Commons
H.L.	House of Lords
J.P.	Justice of the Peace
J.R.A.H.S.	Journal of the Royal Australian Historical Society
M.L.	Mitchell Library, Sydney
M.L.A.	Member of the Legislative Assembly
M.P.	Member of Parliament
N.A.	National Archives
N.L.I.	National Library of Ireland
N.S.W.	New South Wales
N.U.I.	National University of Ireland
O.P.	Outrages Papers
P.R.O.	Public Record Office, London
R.M.	Resident Magistrate
T.A.B.	Tithe Applotment Books

Figures

Ireland 1830

Donegal

Aghadowey · · Armoy

Derry

Antrim

· Belfast

Tyrone

Benburb ·

Fermanagh

Armagh

Down

Monaghan

Sligo

Leitrim

Cavan

· Dundalk

Mayo

Roscommon

Longford

Louth

Hollymount ·

Meath

Galway

Westmeath

Dublin

· Dublin
· Kingstown

King's
County

Kildare

· The Curragh

Queen's
County

Wicklow

Clare

· Nenagh

Tipperary

Carlow

Cashel ·

Kilkenny

Limerick ·

Wexford

Limerick

Moyglass ·

New Ross ·

Clogheen · Clonmel

Killinick ·

Araglen ·

Waterford

Waterford

Kerry

Fermoy ·

Cork

· Cahirciveen

Cork ·

Youghal
· Cove
Spike Island

Waterford & Lismore

- - - - Northern boundary of
united dioceses of
Waterford & Lismore

0   Kilometres   60

0   Miles   40

Chapter 1

Economic and Social Background of the Connerys

On 22 July 1838, in a speech from the dock of Waterford Courthouse, John Connery identified the major cause of turmoil within Irish society as being the robbery of the poor by the rich.[1] He further added that he had done nothing which would raise a blush on his forehead. This apologia was delivered at the culmination of a prolonged, violent conflict between the brothers Patrick, James and John Connery and the authorities. This conflict, which had an enormous impact on the Waterford of the 1830s, involved murder, forcible possession of land and escapes from prison. It led, eventually, to the transportation of the Connerys to New South Wales.

John Connery and his brothers had done little wrong in the eyes of the small farmers and labourers of the Comeragh foothills. The Connerys had fulfilled what they saw as their social obligations in the crucial area of land possession by attempting to implement the common law,[2] in a spectacular way:

'Is go bhfuil 'fhios ag gach aoinne nach rabhadar ciontach riamh in aon choir,
Ach ag seasamh 'na gceart féineach is gan é acu le fáil.[3]
(Everyone knows they were above reproach,
Fighting only for their rights which were denied).

In this society, particularly in the 1830s, land was of vital importance. In their endeavours to reinforce the principle that landholding involved more than a financial contract between tenant and landlord, the Connerys were perceived as rendering vital community service. The perpetrators of agrarian violence invariably reaped the whirlwind but their communities benefited from the salutary effects on local land distribution. Beresford Boate, J.P. of Tournore, Dungarvan and Pierce Hely, J.P. of Rockfield, Cappagh, were witnesses before an inquiry into the conditions of the poorer classes in Ireland in the mid 1830s. They discerned a new climate of reality among landlords, a concentration of minds, which Connery action had helped to induce.

The fear of causing an extension of distress has in some instances prevented junction of farms, and the fear of outrage now prevents such

1

junction ... (Mr. Hely added) Until the last three or four years a good number of tenants were ejected, but now the landlords are afraid.[4]

Thomas Foley, attorney, land agent and sometime sub-sheriff of County Waterford, who was the Connerys' great protagonist, shared in this learning process also. In 1842 he answered criticism that he was not doing enough about the cottier problem on Lord Midleton's Irish estates by stating:

> You do me wrong in supposing that I am not impressed with the injury the landlord sustains in having his land covered with cottier tenants. I am as fully aware of it as anyone can be and the number which I have removed during the last three years affords strong evidence on the subject. Indeed, I omit no opportunity of getting rid of them, but my long experience in the management of property in this country points out the necessity of doing so in the manner least objectionable to the habits and prejudices of the people.[5]

At first sight the Connerys appear to be no different from those who were involved in the mainstream of agrarian violence between 1750 and the Famine, the Whiteboy tradition of Michael Beames.[6] What set them apart was the extraordinary manner in which they articulated, personalised and made explicit that tradition. Initially they had taken advantage of its anonymity,[7] but when their identities were discovered they did not try to avoid the publicity. When confronted by the magistracy, the police and the courts, they were defiant and, particularly in the case of John, contemptuous to the end. Moreover their intelligent manipulation of the judicial system undermined the system from within. This subversion reached its climax in John Connery's 'I'll return to you again Mr. Foley',[8] after he had been sentenced for withholding forcible possession from the landlord. The system has been turned on its head – the convict pronounces on his prosecutor.

The impact on local society was tremendous and the Connerys assumed the heroic mantle of Oisín:

> Dá siúlfainn tír na hÉireann, Sasana le chéile,
> Alba, Van Diemen, an Éigipt is an Spáinn,
> Is geallaimse gan bhréag daoibh nach raghad ag insint éithigh,
> Nach bhfaighinn a neart ná a dtréineacht in aon bheirt deartháir.[9]
> (If you travelled all Ireland and England as well
> Spain, Egypt, Scotland and more could I tell
> That nowhere could you find without falsehood or lies
> The power and the strength of those two brave boys.)

Just as the ancient Gaelic poets depicted Oisín as defending his world against Patrick's Christian Ireland, the Connerys were seen as attempting to validate the mores of their own society against the dominant orthodoxy. Since the struggle was so unequal and they, like Oisín, had to rely on their wits and intelligence, any success reflects as much on the character of their own society as on themselves.

The Connerys' enemies saw them as renegades who had reneged on their social obligations. They were considered to belong to the more prosperous classes, even though it appears they owned, at most, twenty six acres of land. This perception was reinforced by journalists: not alone had the Connerys 'been of the better class of farmer',[10] but 'they were once in circumstances more favourable than generally fell to the lot of the peasantry'.[11] Even Judge Joy at the Waterford County Assizes alluded to their respectability.[12] Their activities, therefore, were seen as disloyal or even traitorous, placing at risk the right of a citizen to dispose of his property as he liked. Moreover, Whigs, Tories, Radicals and Repealers all agreed that men of property governed society and, therefore, it followed that only deviants from this class could really threaten society. Further, they feared that Whiteboys and their ilk might rally around charismatic leaders such as the Connerys. Baron William Cusack, the controversial judge, warned against that danger, in an address to the Grand Jury of Tipperary.[13] 'Who then were these Connerys?'.

Patrick, James and John Connery, brothers, were born in 1797, 1806 and 1808, respectively. They were natives of the townland of Bohadoon in the County of Waterford. Bohadoon lies within the civil parish of Kilgobinet, in the Barony of Decies Without Drum, on the slopes of the Monavullagh Mountains. It lies about six miles northwest of Dungarvan, fourteen miles southeast of Clonmel and eighteen miles southwest of Carrick-on-Suir. It is an upland situation, consisting of open mountain to the north and the deep glen of the Colligan river to the south. Bohadoon, then, contained some woodland and there was also some wood cover on the sides of the glen. The pattern of settlement as depicted on the 1841 Ordnance Survey six inch map is dispersed,[14] although the *clachan* or farmhouse cluster still prevailed in some parts of the Comeragh uplands.[15] To the west lies the civil parish of Seskinane also known as Sliabh gCua, the cultural traditions of which used to pervade most of the surrounding parishes. The Connerys did not escape its influences.

Ancient Sliabh gCua consisted of the territory bounded by the Galtee, Knockmealdown and Comeragh mountain ranges, respectively. Later, it was confined to the area between the Knockmealdowns and the Comeraghs and to the civil parishes of Seskinane and Lickoran, in particular. A semi-circle can be drawn about Seskinane and Lickoran to designate Sliabh gCua's cultural hinterland – the civil parishes of St. Mary's, Inislounaght, Kilronan, Newcastle, Modeligo, Kilgobinet and Colligan. Moving inwards from the circumference, the flat lands of the Suir and Finisk valley floors soon gives way to the uplands and foothills of the Comeragh and its sister the Monavullagh mountain ranges. Sliabh gCua may be translated into English as 'rough mountain'.[16]

The poor, hilly soils of Sliabh gCua ensured that it could never become a target for English settlement while more desirable alternatives existed in the fertile soils of the Blackwater and Bride river valleys, and in South Tipperary. The lament of law administrators, in the 1830s, about the absence of resident gentlemen was well founded. The political turmoil and associated land settlements of the seventeenth century had destroyed the power of the McGraths of Sliabh gCua and the O'Briens of Comeragh. Even so, the McGraths, in their eighteenth century reduced status as middlemen, still provided the liberal, cultural, patronage which so delighted the local poet Donncha Rua:

> *Nó ar Shliabh geal gCua rug buaidh na féile*
> *Ag riar lucht duanta, druadh agus cleireach,*
> *I bhfochair Ui Mhodhráin fonn-áird, leigheannta*
> *do dheanfadh sear-dán ós cionn chláir m'eaga*
> (In bright Slieve Gua, the generous handed
> Where priests and poets my tales demanded –
> Or with William O'Moran for song e'er famous,
> Who'd sing our *caoine* when death o'ercame us -)[17]

The Fitzgeralds of Dromana provided a different type of continuity. As Irish Protestants they managed to preserve their lands in the area until the mid-eighteenth century, when they sold a large portion to the Dawson and Holmes families. Through marriage and a change in name to Villiers, the anglicisation of the family became complete. Sliabh gCua and its environs were at the poorer, outer margin of an estate which took up a large part of the Barony of Decies Without Drum, together with a portion of Coshmore and Coshbride. Consequently, Sliabh gCua escaped many of the vagaries of estate management and tenurial arrangements had a tendency to last longer. This was the reason for the position of the McGraths.

Thus Donncha Rua found in Sliabh gCua a culturally homogeneous society, distinguished by its appetite for Irish poetry and a cultural assurance that almost bordered on arrogance. This is epitomised by William O'Moran's Latin epitaph for his sister, a local poetess, 'There were nine Muses in Greece, but the tenth lies beneath this stone'.[18]

It was complimented by constant support for hedge schools which provided popular education, within the limits of the masters' fees, until the early nineteenth century.[19] In 1787, the Protestant Bishop of Waterford and Lismore lamented the idiosyncratic nature of local education: 'In Seskinan the Romanists will not allow the Vicar to keep a Protestant schoolmaster, to whom he offers £6 a year'.[20]

John Connery was a product of this system and so became part of a fortunate, educated minority.[21] He thus imbibed a definite, intellectual tradition and the education he acquired would have enhanced his employ-ment opportunities, the vital importance of which will become apparent later.

While never 'Lords of Sliabh gCua', the Connerys had a long association with that part of West Waterford. There are records of their presence in that area from as far back as the sixteenth century. These records indicate that the family was of superior standing in the region. Charles Smith, writing in 1746, stated that they were one of the principal families in County Waterford.[22] This is clear from an examination of the pardons granted by Elizabeth I (1558-1603) to her rebellious Irish subjects. The Connerys are listed among the pardoned horsemen or yeomen, usually in the retinue of the Fitzgeralds of Dromana. The property of David Og O'Connery at Ballyhanebeg, about two miles east of Cappoquin, was the subject of one of King James's inquisitions in 1619. David's son Donell, gentleman, achieved a certain notoriety on the outbreak of the Civil War in 1641, when it was alleged that he had stolen some corn. While a prisoner, he is reported to have said, 'that the Protestants were trayterous English doggs, and that they knew no god yet they had'.[23] Retribution followed when his 120 acres were declared forfeit to the Commonwealth and he was awarded a transplanter's certificate in 1653/4. In spite of this, Daniel Connery, a gentleman of Drumro[e], a townland adjacent to Ballyhanebeg, made a contribution to Charles II's Irish subsidy in 1662. It may well have been that Donell either returned or else managed to avoid enforced migration.

In Pender's *Census of Ireland* (c. 1659) the name is most common in the Barony of Decies, later subdivided into Decies Within Drum and Decies Without Drum.[24] In keeping with the observed pattern of Catholic families seeking to circumvent religious bars to the accumulation of wealth and property at home (the Penal Laws), Patrick O'Conry of Dungarvan became the progenitor of the O'Conrys of Seville, Spain.[25] In the eighteenth century the Connery family of Loskeran (civil parish of Ardmore) and Coolnasmear (the townland adjacent to Bohadoon) provided successive parish priests (1729-82) of Holy Trinity Without in Waterford city. Family transactions in the Registry of Deeds, wills and the endowment of the Connery burse in the Irish College in Paris testify to their economic well being. Although much of the Connery wealth was later to be dissipated or dispersed, the memory remained.

In the oral tradition, there are three songs which illustrate this. For example:

Gur tógadh iad go gléasta le scoil agus le léamh iad,
nó
Tógadh iad go buachach, gan achrann gan chruatan.[26]
(They were reared in style with reading and writing
or
Their rearing was honourable without strife or privation).

The Bohadoon brothers are afforded a childhood that would befit the nineteenth century representatives of a distinguished family.

What was the extent of this Connery patrimony by the 1830s? Any attempt to establish land distribution in the third and fourth decades of the nineteenth century is subject to the limitation of the Tithe Applotment. The particularly invidious tithe on potatoes had been discontinued by the Tithe Composition Act of 1823 and, therefore, the applotment does not include the labourers and cottiers. Thus, the picture of landholding is not fully complete. However, it is possible to use the 1831 census to discover the percentage of labourers in the population. The Tithe Applotment of 1829 for the civil parish of Kilgobinet lists among the tenants of Miss Holmes, in Bohadoon, a joint tenancy of twenty six acres occupied by Mary Lynch and Patrick Connery.[27] This holding comprised ten acres of second class land, twelve acres of third class land and four acres of fourth class land (the higher the class the greater the tithe liability). It it not unlikely that this Patrick Connery is the father of the Connerys. At the Waterford Summer Assizes of 1835, where John and Patrick (Junior) were indicted for keeping forcible possession of five acres of the lands of Bohadoon, it is mentioned that their father was a tenant of Lord Yarborough and another gentleman who were acting as trustees.[28] Bohadoon had formed part of the Irish estate of Sir Leonard Thomas Worsley Holmes, but, on his death in 1825, it passed into their hands acting presumably on behalf of his daughters, Elizabeth and Emily Ann, who were co-heirs.[29]

The Tithe Applotment Books for Seskinane and Lickoran, 1834 and Kilgobinet and Colligan, 1827, respectively, provide a picture of the Connerys' neighbours.[30] It is clear that small farmers were a significant part of that community. Moreover, it is likely that the Connery position within this grouping should be based on an adjusted holding of thirteen acres, for there is no obvious family connection in the jointholding of Patrick Connery and Mary Lynch. Within Bohadoon such a holding placed them firmly among the smaller farmers – twelve of the townland's seventeen holdings were larger. Alone, such a farm could sustain only one brother in the economic status of their father and childhood. Supplementary employment was essential, therefore, if the brothers were to survive. In this respect they were successful, initially, at least.

In 1829 this Connery land fulfilled a vital function in preserving the Connery social identity, it provided a very tangible link with an illustrious past. That identity could not survive its loss or further diminution even within the particular confines of Sliabh gCua.

The system of landholding in Sliabh gCua had been dominated by middlemen but by 1836 they accounted only for about 450 acres in Kilgobinet, about 400 in Seskinane and none at all in Colligan and Modeligo. In the parishes of Kilgobinet and Seskinane, there was still no resident gentlemen farmers. The tenurial arrangement was such that all the civil parish of Seskinane was held in life-leases, renewable forever.

Similarly in Modeligo, with 600 to 700 acres held by tenants at will. In Colligan leases in one life, or twenty one years, were most common as in Kilgobinet where there were no life-leases renewable forever, but about 1,500 acres were occupied by tenants at will.[31] The land agent was the key figure in the system and was alienated at a tenant's peril.

The breach between Thomas Foley and the Connerys developed over a long period. It arose out of a clash between the agent's sound financial management of the estate and the individual welfare of the Connerys. Ultimately, it was to have the most serious consequences for the Connerys.

The continuation of a particular Connery ethos depended heavily on access to supplementary employment, not alone to provide livelihoods for the brothers whom the farm could not support, but to generate the income that would ensure that the vital land holding could be retained. In any event, two of the brothers, probably John and James, secured positions on the Holmes Estate. There is conflicting evidence as to whether they were employed as woodrangers or labourers. It is more probable that they were woodrangers given John's literacy.[32] Employment such as this guaranteed a steady income as well as providing opportunities to add to stocks of food and fuel – a valuable perk.

The Connerys' good fortune did not last, however. In a series of events, the Connerys lost their positions and were replaced by a Maurice Hackett who as the new woodranger proceeded to prosecute them for stealing timber. A more complete social humiliation could not be imagined. When confronted with the frightening spectre of a *spailpín fánach* (itinerant labourer) future they resorted to drastic measures.

Early on 19 April 1831, two men dressed in women's clothing and with their faces blackened, waylaid Maurice Hackett near his home. One of them fired at him, but the shot was deflected by the buttons on his coat. Then they beat him with gunbutt and stones and left him for dead. Hackett did not die, though he was severely injured, and managed to reach a neighbour's house.[33] This incident, with the attackers dressed as women, is typical of the Whiteboy assassinations described by Beames and was recognised by the wider community as such.[34]

The authorities were in little doubt as to the culprits and John and James Connery were charged, before John Nugent Humble of Cloncoskeran and Beresford Boate, magistrates, with having assaulted Hackett and fired at him with intent to kill, and were committed to the County Gaol in Waterford city.[35] They did not stay there long, for it was the Spring Assizes of 1835 before a prosecution could be sustained against them.

The shooting of Maurice Hackett underlined the vulnerability of the Connerys to the economic parameters that bound them. It marked the first stage in the merciless convergence of these parameters which would ultimately destroy the brothers.

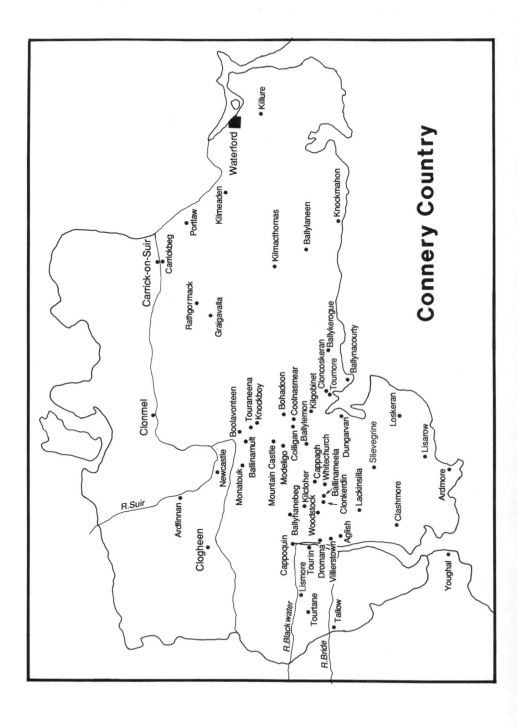

Connery Country

Chapter 2

Connerys under Threat

The Connerys' battle to preserve a particular social identity took place within an environment of economic pressure, social turmoil and widespread political change.

Between 1831 and 1834, a combination of poor potato crops and a significant decline in grain prices, following the fairly satisfactory years of the late 1820s, precipitated severe distress in the countryside.[1] In 1829 the potato harvest had been particularly bad in Waterford and successive poor harvests in the early thirties heightened fears of ruin and hunger among labourers and small farmers. Furthermore, the labourers of Waterford and Tipperary found that they were being undercut on the labour market by more desperate migrants from Cork and Kerry. The locals attempted to institute a pogrom at Carrick-on-Suir on 19 October 1834, but luckily the Cork and Kerrymen gained sanctuary in a shop.[2]

Demographic pressure lead to increased utilisation of marginal land, but the disposal of the *reaghs* (upland heaths) generated further tension within the rural community. Landlords, graziers, cottiers, small farmers and labourers often found themselves in conflict over the fate of the former commonages. The pattern of agrarian outrage in areas like Brow Mountain (Seskinane/Lickoran), Boolavonteen (Seskinane), Scart Mountain (Modeligo) and Slievegrine Mountain (Ardmore) showed that different social groupings were involved. The incidents varied from the spontaneous combustion of turf and new dwellings, the houghing of animals and the traditional levelling of the landlord fencing.[3]

By far the most extraordinary manifestation of this social turmoil were the factions. These had a particular attraction for the small farmers and labourers of the Comeragh uplands so that the impact of the Poleens (*Na Póil*) and Gows (*Na Gaibhne*) of the early 1830s was as marked as that of their more notorious predecessors, the Caravats (*Na Carabhait*) and the Shanavests (*Na Seanabheastaí*).[4] The Connerys, who had experienced the halcyon days of the Caravat movement in their childhood, became prominent members of the Poleens.

9

Roberts has made a social analysis of these archetypal factions and concluded:

> The older feuds were largely territorial, but the new fighting often reflected more modern tensions... In Caravatism one detects a definite heightening of class consciousness among the poor, and Shanavestism shows that the phenomenon was not confined to the poor alone. The Shanavests were an unprecedented middle class anti-Whiteboy movement formed specifically to combat the Caravats.[5]

He sees Caravatism as a product of the wartime agricultural boom of 1793-1813, which affected the market agricultural economy directly by increasing the demand for food. This, in turn, lead to higher prices and greater profits which inflated land values and, as a consequence, rents rose. While this benefited greatly those with secure access to land, it placed new pressures on those at the bottom of the economic scale, particularly the landless.

In Sliabh gCua, the Caravat movement, under the local leadership of Tomás Ó Foghlu of Knockboy, became 'particularly energetic' in the period 1806 to 1809.[6] Ó Foghlu's group was able to convert the cohesion generated by joint tenancies and the institution of communal co-operation (the *meitheal*), into a tightly-knit gang, led by a charismatic leader, who attempted to enforce the Caravat gospel in 'the rich agricultural district of the south, around the ports of Cappoquin and Dungarvan and the village of Aglish'.[7] They attempted to regulate the workings of the market economy by insisting that social considerations be taken into account when conacre, rents and labourers wages were being set.[8] Their success was short-lived and Tomás Ó Foghlu, along with his band, perished at the end of a rope at Knockboy in 1809.

The Dublin Castle authorities were not interested in sociological distinction between Shanavest and Caravat, they viewed them all as potential 'Boneys' men.

More than a generation had elapsed before the Poleens and Gows achieved prominence, in the first half of the early 1830s. While the names had changed, the faction battlegrounds and geographical distribution remained unaltered. Poleen and Gow partisans stretched from Newcastle to Fourmilewater, including the civil parishes of Modeligo, Seskinane and Kilgobinet; mid-Waterford strongholds of Ballylaneen and Kilmacthomas; and the Carrick-on-Suir circle, including Carrickbeg, Rathgormack, Portlaw and Kilmeaden.

As a traditional form of social organisation, the factions could match the excitement and participation which political mobilisation offered the masses in pursuit of Emancipation, Tithe Reform and Repeal. Moreover, in the factions one was not constrained to be a mere follower of the landed gentry, upper middle class and clerical leadership who gathered in

10

Dungarvan Courthouse and Cummins Hotel, Waterford to decide the cures for Ireland's problems. Membership of the faction meant direct participation in all its activities and guaranteed the opportunity to influence those activities. It offered to the small farmers and labourers of the Comeragh uplands a concerted social response to economic upheaval and to those in dire predicaments, like the Connerys, hope.

There is no evidence of any involvement in conventional politics on the brothers' part, despite an indirect contribution to the Waterford County Gaol scandal of 1835.[9] Tradition was of little use in the expensive world of Irish politics. A family which once controlled resources sufficient to guarantee a position of political leadership, by 1830 could not even command a vote in a county election. Thus, for the Connerys, Poleen membership meant access to a leadership role just as the family's declining fortunes excluded them from others.

This, in turn, introduced new risks for the Connerys. The factions threatened the consensus which allowed an upper and middle class Catholic leadership to mobilise the masses in pursuit of non-divisive issues, like Emancipation, Tithes and Repeal.[10] Further, the Poleens and Gows appeared to be beyond clerical control.[11] In appearing impervious to existing social control, the factions' potential for destabilisation was immense. These features, combined with the Connerys' obvious disregard for the law of torts (which ultimately safeguarded the interests of the Catholic landed gentry and upper middle classes), ensured that the harshest judgements on the Connerys' actions were delivered in the *Waterford Chronicle* newspaper, the mouthpiece of the new Catholic political leadership.

If the brothers were not conspicuous enough already, Poleen membership drew further attention from the authorities, as the latter attempted to suppress the factions. Significantly, Henry Villiers Stuart of Dromana, the chief advocate of strong measures against the factions, was the man whose famous victory in the County Waterford election of 1826 inaugerated a new political era. Stuart's (the Liberal, Protestant landlord candidate of the Catholic Association) defeat of Lord George Beresford (the candidate of the great magnate, the Marquis of Waterford) marked the emergence of the new Catholic political leadership.[12]

> By 1835 all 5 seats in Waterford (two in the county, two in the city and one in Dungarvan) were won by anti-Tories, most of whom were even Catholic. The great strides taken towards reform and democratic representation were nowhere highlighted so clearly as they were in the politics of Waterford.[13]

Henry Villiers Stuart's genuine popularity was not tarnished by his opposition to Repeal. He managed to preserve the image of an honest broker on the popular side, though, constrained by his ties with the government and his holding of the office of Lord Lieutenant of the County. He handled a potential political scandal – the Waterford County Gaol inquiry of 1835 – with ease. He was one of the first to alert the government to the serious threat posed by the Poleens and Gows and recommended measures to control and suppress those factions. Significantly, when the Connerys were looking for a pardon from the government, they asked him to mediate.

The response of the authorities to the factions was slow. By 1833 the County Waterford magistracy were becoming aware of the deteriorating conditions of what had been a peaceful county. Their reaction was tempered by financial considerations, however. They wanted to avoid the burden which an increased number of police and a salaried (resident) magistrate would put on the county cess (rates). The 1822 County Constabulary Act required a local financial contribution to law enforcement. It was thought that this would energise the local magistrates and give all citizens a personal, financial interest in reducing crime.

Events, however, were to convince the magistrates that personal safety should take precedence over financial stringency. On 11 February 1833 the Poleens staged a massive show of strength at the fair of Kilgobinet. A group of 500, some with guns, encountered no opposition and rounded off their day by raiding homes for arms.[14] It is inconceivable that the Connerys were not present among the Poleens, given that Bohadoon was but four miles away.

By this action the Poleens not only committed a flagrant breach of public order, they also interfered with a valuable property right. In frightening off business they deprived the owners of the fair, the Musgraves of Tourin, of their fees.

The initial response of the magistracy arose out of a special meeting, on 23 February 1833. The result was a clamp down on unlicensed firearms, tougher licensing for the sale of spirits (restricted to quarter or special sessions); and the vetting of quarry managers as to their fitness to hold gunpowder certificates.[15] These measures had no effect as was underlined by a major eruption of Poleen/Gow violence in October 1833 which resulted in John Connery again coming to the attention of the authorities.

The trouble began on the night of 29 December 1833, when John Heffernan, 'a notoriously bad character', and Poleen leader, was severely beaten by Thomas Thompson in a fight at Ballylaneen.[16] Two days later, the Poleens set out to kill Thompson but were unable to find him. Instead they vented their frustration by smashing several of the village's windows. The outlook for the fair of Ballykerogue which was held on 2 October was bad, for it marked the first anniversary of the performance of elaborate manoeuvres by 300 Poleens. On that occasion, despite a massive security presence, one man was killed in violence after the fair.[17]

Sir John Nugent Humble, with the military and police, arrived on the scene too late to prevent an assault on Patrick Brien. He had been pursued by a group of Poleens who beat him with sticks. The presence of Fr. Thomas Morrissey was insufficient to deter the Poleens and the speed of events prevented him from interfering.[18] Despite medical attention Patrick Brien died of his injuries on 18 October 1833. Chief Constable Francis Crossley of Dungarvan took his death bed declaration, in which he named John Connery as one of his assailants. In like manner, another apparent casualty of the Poleen/Gow feud, David Tobin, who was felled by a stone thrown from behind a ditch, on 5 October 1833, implicated John Connery.[19] Tobin and his wife had been drinking with John and James Connery in Vales' public house, at Colligan Pike. On their way home, Tobin was attacked and received the blow which killed him.

In a pattern which was to become familiar, John Connery proved difficult for the authorities to apprehend. They had greater success at the fair of Carrick-on-Suir, on 17 October 1833, when they arrested twenty seven men, following a spectacular clash between the factions.[20] Twenty two of the prisoners were examined by the magistrates at Dungarvan and six were indicted for the murder of Patrick Brien at Ballykerogue. The others were charged with riot and assault at Carrick.[21] In spite of this, October 1833 closed with an attack by a group of Poleens on two men in Monatook, in the civil parish of Seskinane.[22] By then, however, the scale of violence had finally convinced a majority of magistrates to request the costly assistance of a resident magistrate (R.M.), to be stationed at Dungarvan. The government complied and Sylvanus Jones was transferred from Mayo in early November 1833.

At this stage, there was a real danger that the unrest could evolve into Ribbonism, with the magistrates as the chief targets. The similarities with the activities of the Terry Alts, in Clare (1831) and Tipperary (1832), and the then current Blackfeet/Whitefeet disturbances in Kilkenny were not lost on the landed gentry.

By the end of November 1833, John Connery was apprehended and remanded in the County Gaol to face charges of manslaughter and murder.[23] He faced trial by jurymen who could be expected to have little sympathy for a Poleen – the factions were one area where a consensus existed between the old ascendancy and the new Catholic political leadership.

At the same time Chief Constable Francis Crossley was making great efforts to sustain a successful prosecution in the Patrick Brien case. He arranged to have the two crown witnesses, Catherine Curreen (sister of Patrick Brien) and William McGrath (a young carter), transferred to Dublin, to protect them from intimidation or even death. However, Catherine Curreen would not leave her young family nor William McGrath his

13

business. In McGrath's case, he maintained that since the deposition he had lodged with the magistrates was secret, he had nothing to fear.[24] Crossley had to do the best he could to protect them himself, to the extent of supporting Catherine, who was very poor, in Dungarvan. His efforts were in vain, for their testimony at the Spring Assizes of 1834 proved to be disastrous for the crown case.

The resulting triumph of John Connery, in the face of hostile public opinion and in spite of the best efforts of the forces of law and order, enhanced the mystique of the Connerys still further.

Chapter 3

Trials

At the opening of the 1834 Spring Assizes for County Waterford, Chief Baron Joy sentenced nine of the Poleen and Gow prisoners from the Carrick-on-Suir affray to two years imprisonment.[1]

On Thursday, 6 March 1834, John Connery was put on trial for the murder of David Tobin. He was defended by the Recorder of Waterford, William Henry Hassard, whose able and skilled defence was such that Judge Joy, in his address to the jury:

> expressed a hope that the prisoner should receive the benefit of their doubts, as the principle of the law would rather allow 99 guilty to escape than to punish one innocent man.[2]

David Tobin and his wife Johanna, of Colligan, had gone, with their horse, to Dungarvan to sell a bag of oats. On the homeward journey they were joined by James Connery and Stephen Hanrahan. Stephen Hanrahan asked David Tobin the deadly and controversial question whether he belonged to the Poleens or Gows. Tobin replied that he belonged to neither. The party went into Vales' public house, where they were joined by Gabriel Walsh and John Connery. After drinking a few glasses of whiskey they all left together. James Connery and Johanna Tobin rode ahead on the horse, with the main group following on foot. They had gone only a mile when Tobin was hit by a stone which was thrown from over the ditch. Tobin, on being taken to Gabriel Walsh's house, stated John Connery had killed him.

Johanna Tobin stated that John Connery had threatened her husband at some time during the harvest and had confirmed his declaration in Walsh's. Gabriel Walsh testified that at the fatal moment he was in front of Tobin, by a few paces. Tobin was flanked by Stephen Hanrahan on his left and John Connery on his right. Walsh also twice heard Tobin accuse John Connery of the deed. James Tobin, David's brother, was present at his death and was told, by his brother, that he, David, had seen John Connery go to the ditch on the left, remove a stone and then throw it from the right. When Judge Joy put this crucial piece of evidence to Gabriel Walsh, Walsh confirmed that such a manoeuvre would have been impossible without him observing it. David Tobin, on his deathbed, had told Constable Sheehy that Connery had struck him but, significantly, that Hanrahan had not done so. Sheehy also added that it was only by chance that John Connery was apprehended while on his way to Clonmel, two months after David Tobin's death.

James Connery, for the defence, tried to convey an impression of his brother as a concerned and, by implication, an innocent man. In the end, the jury required only a minute to return a verdict of not guilty.

John Connery and eight others were then put on trial for the manslaughter of Patrick Brien at Ballykerogue. The crown's case disintegrated as the trial progressed. The star witness, William McGrath, developed a complete mental block and was unable to remember identifying four of the prisoners in the presence of Chief Constable Crossley, shortly after Brien's death. Mr. Scott K.C. the prosecutor, pointed out the defendant, Michael Crotty, to him. McGrath's reply was masterful in its sophistry: 'If he is the man I saw at Mr. Crossley's he is'.[3] However, this earned him a sentence of eighteen months for perjury at the Summer Assizes.

Catherine Curreen, the dead man's sister, identified some of the prisoners as having struck her brother, but destroyed her credibility when she identified one John Mullowney as Mooney, a person whom she had known for four years. When James Bruce, the gaoler of the County Gaol, testified that John Mullowney was in his custody on the day of the assault Catherine Curreen was turned off the witness stand. All that remained was the dying declaration of Patrick Brien – that John Connery and John Barrett, a dancing master, had struck him. Constable Sheehy had translated this into English and Chief Constable Crossley had written it down, in the presence of Robert Longan, J.P. of Ballynacourty. The jury was suspicious, however, and asked the hapless Sheehy to retranslate the English document into Irish. He failed to do so. The jury then rejected the document as valid evidence. After a short consultation, the jury found all prisoners not guilty. 'Thus in one day John Connery was acquitted of a charge of murder, and a charge of manslaughter'.[4]

In his own community John became a celebrity as one of the few who had survived the rigours of the Irish judicial system, but this reprieve was to be of a temporary nature. That system was yet to bring John and his brothers to 'justice' and John's singular good fortune would not disprove the French political commentator, Gustave de Beaumont's dictum:

> In England, the magistrate sees in every accused person an unfortunate fellow citizen, a person charged with a crime of which he may be innocent, an Englishman invoking the sacred rights of the constitution. In Ireland, the justices of the peace, the judges, and the jury, treat the accused as a kind of idolatrous savage, whose violence

must be subdued, as an enemy that must be destroyed, as a guilty man destined beforehand for punishment.[5]

John Connery was no sooner reunited with his family than they had to face the serious threat posed by Thomas Foley, of Tourtane, Lismore, in the Barony of Coshmore and Coshbride, land agent, landowner, solicitor and sometime sub-sheriff.[6]

The Barony of Coshmore and Coshbride contains the most fertile land in all Waterford, along the flat river valleys of the Blackwater and its tributary, the Bride. The numerous demesnes testified to its attractiveness for the Ascendancy. Here there was no shortage of resident gentlemen. In contrast to the Comeragh uplands, farms were large and the strength of the small farmers and labourers weak. The Caravats had achieved transitory success here but the Poleens never managed to make their presence felt. Secure in this knowledge, the magistrates and ratepayers of the barony had objected strongly to the appointment of a resident magistrate.

Thomas Foley held the agency for the Holmes Estate. He was a professional gentleman and a member of the Protestant branch of a prominent Lismore family, whose interests embraced land, flour milling and a salmon fishery. Thomas was not the only one to pursue a professional career, two others followed in his footsteps as attorneys, another member became a surgeon. Indeed, Edmond Foley would serve continuously as sub-sheriff of the county from 1837 to his death in 1860.

Thomas Foley belonged to the efficient breed of land administrators who sought more economic utilisation of the land. Invariably, this involved the displacement of the small farmers and cottiers and their replacement by larger units under the care of good i.e. improving tenants – a replication of the distribution of land in Coshmore and Coshbride.[7] However, such a process could provoke a drastic reaction from tenants fearful of being surplus to the new requirements, as Beames has demonstrated in the case of County Tipperary.[8]

Thomas Foley was, therefore, in the position of having to deal with the infamous Connerys if only to overawe the other tenants. The Connerys treatment of Maurice Hackett and membership of the Poleens was indicative of their understanding of the rights of property. Foley decided to evict them, but the precise grounds on which he did so are unclear: accounts of the trial of Patrick and John at the Summer Assizes of 1835 cite the euphemism 'misconduct',[9] while the sensational 'Interesting Particulars of their Extraordinary Escapes and Adventures' maintains it was simply because of the accumulation of arrears of rent.[10]

Thomas Foley followed the correct legal procedure and secured a decree for their ejectment on 24 June 1834. John Connery responded by threatening Foley if he were to attempt to execute the decree. Nevertheless, the sub-sheriff accompanied by a large police escort oversaw a bloodless eviction and the Connerys did not resist. Instead, Mr. Foley received the following letter in the mail:

> Mr. Thomas Foley I am credibly informed that you main, to distraine your tinnents in Bohodoone assure you that if you dont Chaing your mind to the reverse that you will surely suffer first & foremost your woods will be consumed to ashes as for your own life will be in danger for you wont be at home always.
>
> Ballylemon Woods is our object.[11]

He was certain that he could trace the letter to one of the Connerys, probably John. At the Summer Assizes of 1835, he maintained that the Connerys had sworn that they would have opposed the eviction party openly, had they known when they were coming. Instead, they waited until the police force had withdrawn and then threatened the new tenant, who promptly fled. Such a lesson on how to resist evictions was not lost on the Connerys' neighbours and the reputation of the Connerys grew in the same proportion as it deteriorated in the legal world of Thomas Foley. Thomas Foley, who had been a sub-sheriff for four years, was not intimidated, but took an active part in their prosecution for repeated acts of forcible possession and also for the Maurice Hackett affair. He felt that both his life and the economic management of the Holmes estate were at stake and, being a solicitor, he was well qualified to seek legal remedies.

Meanwhile, the pattern of the Poleen and Gow conflict had remained unchanged. A clash at the fair of Knockboy on 14 December 1833 was continued in the chapel yard of Touraneena on the following Sunday morning, 'during the celebration of divine service'.[12] At the fair of Mountain Castle on 1 May 1834, they came together in the late evening. When Sylvanus Jones, R.M., accompanied by the military and police, intervened, the mob pelted them with stones, from behind a wall. However Chief Constable Crossley outflanked them and took a number of prisoners, among them Denis Croneen, who was sentenced to one year's imprisonment, at the County Waterford Summer Assizes of 1834. At the corresponding fair for 1837, the Croneens led the Poleens against the McGrath-inspired Gows, whose leader Thomas McGrath received a severe beating.[13] One Denis Croneen was sentenced to death at the County Waterford Summer Assizes of 1839 for conspiracy to murder the landlord John O'Keeffe of Mountain Castle.[14]

Sporting events were not immune to this inexorable conflict. A bull bait at Rathgormack on 16 November 1834 ended in a faction riot which continued until Major Rowan, resident magistrate at Carrick-on-Suir, and the police succeeded in arresting the leaders.[15] While the authorities were able to achieve some success in vigilant policing of the fairs, the personal assassinations which were hallmarks of the feud proved more difficult to anticipate.

Meanwhile, Thomas Foley's judicial pursuit of the Connerys resulted in their apprehension and lodging in the County Gaol. The manner of their capture is unclear but it is probable that it was as described by Tomás Ó Corcoráin, in Seanchas Sliabh gCua:

> Ach cé go raibh cáirde go leór acu, bhí namhaid acu leis. Dhíol duine éigint iad sa tslí gur rugadh orthu agus go cuireadh isteach i bpríosún Phortláirge iad, ...[16]

(And even though they had many friends they also had enemies. One of these turned informer with the result that they were captured and imprisoned in Waterford Gaol ...)

Informing was usually carried out by those who had a grudge against those they betrayed and the mercenary gain only reinforced their moral vindication. The Connerys, with their Poleen profile and social activism, had powerful enemies throughout the whole peasant communities – from fearful, strong farmers to disaffected, 'poor' Gows. The Connerys were to provide much employment for informers.

John Connery's incarceration proved temporary as he managed to forge a bail bond with Robert Longan J.P.'s signature on it and was set free in 1835. Sylvanus Jones R.M. spent £3 on private information which resulted in John's recapture.[17]

On 11 March 1835, at the County Waterford Spring Assizes, James and John Connery were tried for conspiracy to murder Maurice Hackett, and also for firing at him, with intent to kill.

The main witness for the prosecution, Laurence Crotty, was planting cabbages in a field nearby on the day of the attack. In a deposition to Beresford Boate J.P., given in Irish and translated into English, he had stated he had seen John/James Connery strike Hackett. Now he did not know John Connery or see him strike Hackett. He paid for his amnesia – he was sentenced to seven years transportation, for wilful and corrupt perjury.[18] Another witness, Laurence Connell, said that he saw the incident but did not know either of the 'maids'. A third witness, William Foley, who knew both James and John Connery, testified that he had heard James Connery admit that he had fired at Hackett (There must be a suspicion that this Mr. Foley was not unconnected with one Thomas Foley).[19]

Both Connerys were aquitted on the conspiracy charge, but James was convicted of firing with intent to kill. In passing sentence Judge Torrens explained he would have sentenced James to death had the trial followed immediately after the offence. He conceded that the information sworn at the time might not have sustained a conviction and that the passage of time might have encouraged James Connery to make his incriminating statements – thinking he was safe from prosecution. The justice then recorded the sentence of death and James Connery was sentenced to transportation for life. The Judge, in conclusion, stated, 'he trusted and he believed he was doing his duty, but if he erred, it was on the side of mercy'.[20]

For the third and final time John Connery had been acquitted, but James was bound for New South Wales. This left only John and Patrick to face the 'taking forcible possession charge'. A total triumph for Thomas Foley and the society he represented appeared imminent – Ireland's gain would be New South Wales's loss.

The relationship between the Connerys and the Governor of the County Gaol, James Bruce, became the subject of much controversy. Observers as diverse as Fr. Garret Prendergast, the Catholic chaplain and Thomas Foley himself considered Mr. Bruce's conduct unprofessional, at the very least. According to Garret Prendergast, Bruce presided over a 'system of cruelty and oppression unexampled in any civilized country in the World'.[21]

In sixteen detailed charges he sought to expose the harshness of the Bruce regime, with its beatings, its skimming-off of the prisoners' provisions and its tainted water supply. Writing of the dangerous insubordination within the gaol he highlighted the events of 16 April 1835, when an unimpeded riot took place between the prisoners. This subsided into a boxing match between John Connery and a man named Hackett, in which James Connery was brought from another part of the prison to help John. Fr. Prendergast claimed that not alone had Bruce encouraged John, but that he afterwards struck Hackett. The day ended with some of the prisoners [unnamed] consuming meat in the pantry, having been invited there (it was a Catholic feast day).[22]

Scrutator, in a letter to the *Waterford Chronicle*, provided fascinating details of these events. It appears that the riot had arisen because of overcrowding, which resulted in the Poleens being held with the Gows. The Gows, fewer in number, came out worse in this engagement and suggested their dispute be settled by single combat. This resulted in John Connery, for the Poleens, entering the ring against Hackett. When the verdict was given to John, after a contest lasting half an hour which had been distinguished by the cheering of the prison staff, Hackett and his party complained of foul play. As if this were not a serious reflection on prison discipline, Scrutator was particularly disgusted by what followed:

> When peace and order seemed to be restored, the inner gates of the prison were thrown open, and a man named James Connery (brother to John) a convicted felon, was brought forward from another quarter of the gaol. This monster, this desparate bravo, assisted by two bullies who were kept in reserve, were actually let loose on the unfortunate Hacket (sic), and his two brothers, who were now exhausted and weltering in their gore. Connery and his associates were sent back to their cells after they satiated themselves on their mangled victims. It is a fact, that during this conflict many severe

wounds were inflicted on the Hackets with some of the heavy and massive keys which are generally used by the officers of the gaol in unlocking the doors.[23]

An investigation was carried out in which Bruce was chided for his lack of judgement and 'want of discretion' with respect to the riot, but Turnkey Sweeney was blamed for the introduction of James Connery – 'an unjustifiable act' — for which he had been severely reprimanded by the Gaoler. Meat had been eaten by the prisoners but the Gaoler had been unaware of this. The charges relating to beating Hackett and provisions and water were unfounded.[24] Bruce mobilised the written testimony of Protestant dignitaries and numerous magistrates as to his exemplary character. Garret Prendergast had little presumption when he wrote to the Lord Lieutenant Mulgrave, 'I have now to inform your Lordship that the *faction*, the orange faction, are making the most extraordinary exertions to keep the gaoler in his place'.[25]

It was Prendergast, however, who was removed by the Grand Jury and the Lord Lieutenant of the County, Henry Villiers Stuart. A political storm, with strong sectarian overtones, ensued. The Bishop of Waterford and Lismore, Dr. Abraham, maintained that he alone had the authority to remove Fr. Prendergast and proceeded to flay the Grand Jury for attempting such a usurpation of this authority.[26]

When the Grand Jury appointed a new Catholic chaplain, Fr. Michael Fitzgerald P.P., the prisoners in the County Gaol found themselves without spiritual welfare. Garret Prendergast protested his integrity in letters to the *Waterford Chronicle* and sought a public investigation into the affair. The role of Henry Villiers Stuart came into question and he had to take out an advertisement in the *Chronicle* claiming that his behaviour had been proper. He had sent the testimonies of all the witnesses and his own conclusion to the Lord Lieutenant and so considered that everything had been fair.[27] It was alleged, afterwards, that the *bête noir* of the popular party, John Mathew Galwey, had proposed Prendergast's dismissal, but Galwey denied this, saying he had just agreed with all the other Catholics on the Grand Jury.[28] It took the appointment of a compromise chaplain, Dr. Edward Barron, in 1836 to end the affair. He endeavoured to have Garret Prendergast admitted to the Gaol as his assistant, but the Gaol's Board of Superintendence had declared Prendergast *persona non grata*.[29]

Garret Prendergast had attacked an institution of the establishment and suffered accordingly. It was poor reward for a man who maintained that he had frustrated, at much danger to himself, a plot to murder the gaoler and the turnkey. Bruce's successor as Governor, Thomas Ryan, would claim to have discovered and defeated a similar 'horrible' Connery plot in August 1838. It may well have been that Garret Prendergast ended any hope James Connery had of avoiding transportation.

James was marched to Cove and lodged in the hulk *Surprise* from whence, on 24 August 1835, he sailed to New South Wales on board the convict transport *Hive*. The *Hive* was wrecked near Cape St. George but the intrepid James was one of the survivors who landed in Sydney just before Christmas.

At the County Waterford Summer Assizes, on 22 July 1835, Patrick and John Connery were put on trial for taking forcible possession of five acres of land. Their sang-froid was remarked upon: 'These worthies were well acquainted with the Court, and showed by their nonchalence that they were careless of their situation'.[30]

In reality, the Connerys, through Mr. Hassard, had attempted to come to a settlement with the Crown during the morning. If James were to receive a general pardon they would all leave the country. Thomas Foley was outraged, 'you wanted to have a man transported for felony, pardoned?'.[31]

Mr. Hassard then attempted to base the Connerys' defence on the legal technicality that as they had taken 'quiet' possession and then forcibly detained it, the act under which they were charged did not apply. Mr. Scott K.C. for the Crown contended otherwise – the act perfectly comprehended the charge. Mr. Hassard made a final offer in which he stated the if the Connerys were granted a verdict of acquittal he would ensure that they would be out of the country by the next assizes. Mr. Scott had grave doubts as to whether Mr. Hassard could get rid of them and favoured a more pragmatic approach: He 'thought the surest way to get rid of them was to convict them, for he thought it would benefit the country to have them removed'.[32]

The jury were only out a few minutes and returned a verdict of guilty. Chief Baron Joy in sentencing the Connerys, was conscious of his moral and social duties: 'the prisoners have been convicted of a very serious crime, and he hoped the example made of them, as they appeared respectable, would be a warning to others'.[33] He sentenced them to seven years transportation.

John Connery did not accept the verdict – his, 'I'll return to you again Mr. Foley',[34] outburst caused consternation in the courthouse. This social disapproval was echoed most strongly by the reporter of the *Waterford Chronicle:* 'it showed the character of as great a wretch as ever disgraced existence'.

The Catholic middle and upper classes had cogent reasons for fearing the Whiteboy tradition.

Alexis de Tocqueville and Gustave de Beaumont were present at the same assizes, engaged in fact-finding for their analysis of Irish society. De Tocqueville's attention was drawn to the factions – eight men were sentenced to six months hard labour arising out of a Poleen/Gow riot at the fair of Kilmacthomas on 12 May 1835 in which one man died.[35] He brought no new perception to the problem rather he accepted the conventional wisdom, 'Factions which started nobody knows when, and which continue nobody knows why, and take on no political colour'.[36] With de Beaumont, he recognised the vital role of land within Irish society and it is interesting to speculate how much the case of John and Patrick Connery contributed to Gustave de Beaumont's formulation of Irish social realities.

> The peasant must possess a plot of ground, or starve. This is the secret of that extraordinary rivalry of which land is the object in Ireland. The land in the country resembles a fortress eternally besieged and defended with indefatigable ardour; there is no safety unless within its precincts; he who makes good his entrance leads a life of labour, privation, and peril, but still he lives he holds fast to the rampart – he clings to it; and in order to remove him, it is necessary to tear him limb from limb. The condition of the unfortunate who has failed in attaining this object is lamentable; for unless he yields himself to starvation, he must either beg or rob.[37]

The Connerys had finally been precipitated into the social abyss by the legal system and their significance, in the Irish context, should now have ended. If John Connery should ever return again to Thomas Foley his triumph would be as metaphysical as the *lá eile* of Éamonn de Paor.[38]

Lismore Castle, from one of the dry arches under the bridge. Drawn by R. Hill, Esq. Cork.

Chapter 4

Escapes

An extraordinary turn of events ensured that the verdict of the court could not be implemented for over three years. This was because the Connerys spent very little of that time in custody, almost twenty three months of which they were on the run. In two successful escape bids the Connerys regained their freedom and proceeded in attempts to overturn the verdict of the court or alternatively to escape overseas. Both escapes were characterised by the adoption of different strategies to achieve these aims.

On the first occasion the brothers, heavily armed, were very much on the offensive, seeking to overthrow the sentence of the court through violence. As mobile gunmen they posed part of a serious, perennial problem for the Irish Administration – that of such gunmen enforcing and encouraging rural anarchy. In this respect, the Connerys were extremely active so that Dublin Castle was justifiably relieved when they were recaptured.

In contrast the Connerys' final escape took place when the initiative had passed from the brothers. Just as their world was subjected to increasingly more effective social control from the Melbourne Administration, the Connerys found themselves on the defensive. Apparently they decided that violence could not redress so great an imbalance and resorted to other measures. A brilliant innovation gave them a temporary respite, but they eventually settled on achieving a negotiated settlement with the authorities. When this failed the Connerys were doomed, all tactics exhausted, but to no avail.

On 17 August 1835, in the company of James Bruce and a military escort, John and Patrick and two other convicts were marched the twenty five miles to Clonmel, in transit to the hulk *Surprise* at Cove. On the following day, the Clonmel garrison would only provide a military escort as far as Clogheen and not Fermoy, twenty six miles away, as James Bruce had requested. Dublin Castle had rectified this anomaly but fortunately for the Connerys word had not reached Clonmel by 18 August 1835.[1] The military returned to their barracks and the Connerys and the others were lodged in the Clogheen bridewell.

At evening, John Connery requested to go to the privy and when the yard door was opened the prisoners rushed out. The Connerys sprang into action, they jumped the six feet up on to a privy wall and scaled the remaining nine feet of the bridewell wall, to freedom. Their companion, John Noonan, who was not destined for greatness, fell into the privy pit, when he tried to duplicate the Connerys' feat. The Connerys had only to cross the Knockmealdown Mountains and they were home. The gaolers left in their wake proceeded to blame each other for the escape. Marcus Jackson, the bridewell keeper, charged:

> The said Patrick Connery and John Connery having been allowed by the said Bruce to dress themselves in very respectable coloured clothes with seal Skin Caps and Gold bands and tassels.[2]

Moreover he would detail Bruce's drinking on the day. His most serious allegation was however that the Connerys' leg irons were only tied with cord and contained locks of inferior quality. Added to this Bruce did not exert himself in the pursuit even to the extent of calling on the Clogheen constabulary to organise the search.

Bruce countered all these allegations of malpractice. He denied freeing the Connerys of their chains, rather the key was in his pocket at all times further that their dress and haircuts were those proper to convicts at all times. He stated that he found Jackson's conduct during the escape incident inexplicable particularly his opening of the yard door.[3]

Bruce placed a reward of £10 in the *Hue and Cry* (newspaper) for the Connerys' apprehension. However Thomas Foley, armed with Jackson's deposition would have Bruce charged with 'having wilfully permitted the escape of the Convicts John and Patrick Connery', and arraigned for trial at the County Tipperary Spring Assizes of 1836.[4]

Thomas Foley's reaction to the Connerys' escape had been comprehensive and incisive and bore all the hallmarks of a genuinely worried man. By 21 August 1835, from his Dublin office, 178 Great Brunswick Street, he had informed the Under-Secretary of State for Ireland, Thomas Drummond, of the main details of the Connery affair and exerted subtle pressure for official action:

> I do confidently hope that as I have done my duty in bringing these Persons to Justice, that the government will use every effort by rewards and otherwise to have them retaken and the Sentence pronounced on them carried into effect.[5]

Without delay, Foley carried out his own investigation into the circumstances of the Clogheen escape, keeping Dublin Castle informed as he took action against Bruce. He carefully monitored the authorities pursuit of the Connerys and highlighted inadequacies. By 3 October 1835, he was appealing to Michael O'Loghlen, the Attorney-General, as the first law officer of the crown, 'for assistance & protection'.[6] His lobbying was so thorough that he managed to organise a private meeting with Lord Morpeth, the Chief Secretary for Ireland, on the subject. Moreover, Foley got W.S. Curry, the Irish agent of the Duke of Devonshire, to write to Lord Morpeth to reinforce his memory on the affair. This created the impression that Devonshire, an influential Whig, was deeply concerned about the 'professional gentleman' residing upon his property.[7]

It devolved upon Thomas Drummond, the active head of the Irish Administration, to solve the Connery problem which would come to represent just another small fraction of his total responsibility for law and order.

The Melbourne Administration (1835 to 1841) would pursue a policy of unprecedented conciliation towards the Irish majority. The *Waterford Chronicle* described it as 'the first popular Administration that Ireland has ever beheld'.[8]

For the first time the centres of power would become accessible and amenable to the views and aspirations of the Catholic, middle class leadership of the Irish peasantry. Thomas Drummond, the dedicated and gifted young Scottish bureaucrat, has often been cast as the prime mover of this policy. Ó Tuathaigh argues that it was the concerted action of the triumvirate of Lord Mulgrave as Lord Lieutenant, Lord Morpeth as Chief Secretary and Drummond as Under-Secretary which ensured such a policy could take form.[9] The most revolutionary aspect of this policy was the recognition that official repression exacerbated rather than checked underlying political and socio-economic problems. Military and police support were no longer to be the automatic adjunct of a property owner distraining for rent or tithe. Thomas Drummond would tell the Select Committee on Crime in Ireland, 'His Excellency cannot allow their actual presence on the spot till a violation of the peace shall call for it'.[10] This official policy of neutrality helped in small way to reduce violence. Ó Tuathaigh credits this new departure with defusing the Tithe War.[11]

When the County Tipperary magistracy felt threatened in 1838 by what they saw as the re-emergence of agrarian anarchy and applied to the government, in time-honoured fashion, for exceptional measures, Thomas Drummond made the famous reply:

> Property had its duties as well as its rights; to the neglect of these duties in times past is mainly to be ascribed that diseased state of society in which such crimes take their rise; and it is not in the enactment or enforcement of statutes of extraordinary severity, but chiefly in the better and more faithful performance of those duties, and the most enlightened and humane exercise of these rights, that a permanent remedy for such disorders is to be sought.[12]

It comes as no surprise that Thomas Drummond met Gustave de Beaumont and read his analysis of Irish society.

New priorities within Dublin Castle were underlined in the appointment of Irish Catholics to positions of state. Michael O'Loghlen, a barrister and a Whig from County Clare, benefited spectacularly in this regard. As M.P. for Dungarvan he became, successively, Solicitor-General and Attorney-General for Ireland in 1835. John Mathew Galwey's opposition at the by-elections, which resulted from those appointments, made his breach with the popular party irreparable.[13] In 1836, O'Loghlen's appointment as Baron of the Exchequer made him the first Catholic Judge since 1688 in England or Ireland and required him to end his political career. He was appointed Master of the Rolls in 1837 and created a baronet in 1838.

The Irish Constabulary Act of 1836 created an efficient centralised police force, under the total control of the Lord Lieutenant. The local input to policing which had been monopolised by the magistracy was ended. Under the minute supervision of Thomas Drummond, Dublin Castle, could, for the first time, dictate policing policy and implement it directly.

In the pursuit of the Connerys in 1835 the chain of command was Thomas Drummond to Major William Miller, Inspector General of Police for Munster, to Sub-Inspector Samuel Croker the ranking police officer in County Waterford. Its beginnings were not auspicious, although Drummond had authorised a reward of £50 for the recapture of John and Patrick by 1 September 1835, all copies of the proclamation were dispatched to County Tipperary police stations. It required a second printing by the Government printers in November 1835 to rectify the error and provide Major Miller and the County Waterford constabulary with the requisite copies.[14] The Connerys proved to be elusive quarry. In late September 1835 Sub-Inspector Croker, based at Cappoquin, was notified by Constable Hegarty of Villierstown that the Connerys were drinking in Devines' public house, between Aglish and Clashmore. Croker dispatched Constable Major Atkins and a party of constabulary to liaise with Hegarty at Villierstown. Together they raided Devines', but drew a blank. Leaving a guard to prevent the customers leaving, they split their forces in half and surrounded Bransfields' house at Lackinsilla and that of Keeffe's, which was also nearby.[15]

In the swoop on Bransfields' they captured a suit of clothes and a belt. It was assumed Bransfields' maid alerted a sleeping Patrick Connery who escaped through a window in the back of the house. The party went back to Cappoquin with the clothes, which were returned later, on the advice of Sir Richard Keane. Although Croker felt he now had an important lead as to how the Connerys were dressed, his reward of £40 (for private information) was having little effect. Friends of the Connerys were circulating misinformation and he was denied the 'correct information', without which it was impossible to arrest them.[16]

At that time, the Connerys were taking very effective counter measures.

They called to a steward of Thomas Foley's brother, who lived near Dungarvan, and accused him of giving information about them to the police. They put it about that it was through the influence of Sir Richard Keane that they got back their clothes (Keane had property in Ballylemon, quite close to Bohadoon). According to Thomas Foley, they proceeded to threaten both his and his brother's life unless they received a pardon. Moreover, on 29 September 1835 they were drinking and buying drink in the public house at the Turnpike, near Dungarvan. John was armed and Patrick had a new ramrod. Thomas Foley had property and management of property near Dungarvan, 'but since the escape of these men I have never ventured to go there as these Villians would if they had an Opportunity take away my life'.[17]

In such a vein Thomas Foley couched his appeal of 3 October 1835 to Michael O'Loghlen, the Attorney-General, being careful to state that the Connerys' allegations about Sir Richard Keane could not be true. He was disenchanted with Croker's handling of the Lackinsilla affair, but felt that Chief Constable Francis Crossley of Dungarvan was doing his best. He proved no more successful than Garret Prendergast in removing James Bruce from the County Gaol. Though on bail, Bruce continued in his position.

The paradoxical situation is best illustrated in W.S. Curry's letter to Lord Morpeth where he gives Thomas Foley the role of quarry being pursued by the armed Connerys who 'have most violently threatened to take his life, and I believe there is no doubt, have recently being way laying him, with that determination'.[18]

The grim nature of the agrarian conflict was reasserted on 11 October 1835 when an assassination attempt by two men on the landlord John Quinlan of Clonkerdin, Dungarvan failed. Quinlan, a Catholic, later identified the gunman as Patrick Kiely, in the house of James Morrissey, a tenant, whose lease had expired in June and was about to be evicted.[19] Quinlan and the police also discovered some gunpowder and recovered the loaded pistol from the person of Morrissey's wife. At the County Spring Assizes for 1836 Chief Justice Doherty sentenced Kiely and Morrissey to death, the former having been convicted of firing at Quinlan and the latter for aiding and assisting in the same. From the scaffold, on 19 March 1836, Patrick Kiely admitted the deed.[20] Because of a speech impediment Fr. Dooley spoke for James Morrissey and delivered a message against the incipient evil of drinking, intoxication, bad company and gambling. According to the *Waterford Chronicle* both admitted the justness of their sentence.[21] The whole poignant episode thus became an exercise in the reaffirmation of conventional morality as preached by landlord and church.

In consistently protesting their innocence as at the Summer Assizes of

No. 12,591.

The Dublin Gazette.

𝔓𝔲𝔟𝔩𝔦𝔰𝔥𝔢𝔡 𝔟𝔶 𝔄𝔲𝔱𝔥𝔬𝔯𝔦𝔱𝔶.

TUESDAY, SEPTEMBER 8, 1835.

DUBLIN CASTLE,
September 1, 1835.

WHEREAS it has been represented to the Lord Lieutenant, that on Tuesday, the 18th of August ult., John and Patrick Connery, while on their way to the Convict Hulk, at Cove, effected their escape from the Bridewell at Clogheen, in the County of Tipperary :

His Excellency, for the better apprehending and bringing to Justice the abovenamed Individuals, is pleased hereby to offer a Reward of

FIFTY POUNDS

to any Person or Persons who shall, within Six Months from the date hereof, give such Information as shall lead to the apprehension of the said John and Patrick Connery.

By His Excellency's Command,

T. DRUMMOND.

DUBLIN CASTLE,
September 7, 1835.

WHEREAS it has been represented to the Lord Lieutenant, that on the Night of the 3d September, a quantity of Vitriol was thrown on Mr. Abraham Harty, a Baker in Patrick-street, Cork, by some Person unknown :

His Excellency, for the better apprehending and bringing to justice the Perpetrator of the above Outrage, is pleased hereby to offer a Reward of

FIFTY POUNDS

to any Person or Persons who shall, within Six Months from the date hereof, give such Information as shall lead to his apprehension and conviction.

By His Excellency's Command,

T. DRUMMOND.

DUBLIN CASTLE,
September 4, 1835.

THE Lord Lieutenant has been pleased to approve of Evelyn Philip Shirly, Esq , of Lough Tay, Carrickmacross, being appointed a Deputy Lieutenant for the County of Monaghan. —Commission to bear this date.

From the LONDON GAZETTE of Friday, September 4, 1835.

AT the Court at *St. James's*, the 26th day of *August* 1835,
PRESENT,
The KING's Most Excellent Majesty in Council.

WHEREAS by an Act, passed in the third and fourth year of His Majesty's reign, intituled, " An Act for the general regu- " lation of the Customs," it is, among other things, enacted, that goods of places within the limits of the East India Company's charter shall be imported only into such ports of the United Kingdom as shall be approved of by the Lords of the Treasury, and declared by an Order in Council to be fit and proper for such importation.

And whereas the several ports of Whitehaven and Waterford have, with certain limitations, been approved of by the Lords of His Majesty's Treasury for that purpose, His Majesty, by and with the advice of His Privy Council, is thereupon pleased to declare, and it is hereby declared, that the ports of Whitehaven and Waterford are, respectively, fit and proper for the importation of goods from places within the limits of the East India Company's charter, save and except that such ports shall not be deemed fit and proper for the importation of tea until after the first day of July one thousand eight hundred and thirty-six.

And the Right Honourable the Lords Commissioners of His Majesty's Treasury are to give the necessary directions herein accordingly.
C. C. Greville.

Dublin Gazette Reward Notice, 8 Sept. 1835.

1835 and seeking the elusive pardon, the Connerys had to weigh up the consequences of any action against Thomas Foley. Patrick Connery appeared to be conscious of this when, on the night of 17 December 1835, armed with pistol and [short] gun, they went into the house of Sylvester Greaney of Knockane, Whitechurch. John proceeded to beat up Greaney in the presence of a large number of witnesses. Then 'John Connery presented his gun at him, and seemed determined to murder him, but was prevented by his brother Patrick'.[22]

The reason for the attack was that they suspected Greaney of giving information to the police and had used the incident to give public notice of how they would deal with informers. Faced with the drying up of what little information they had been receiving, the authorities opted for exceptional measures. Thomas Drummond informed Major Miller on 21 December 1835:

> His Exellency is of Opinion that it is not very credible to the Police that these Men Should Still be at large: His Exy requests Major Miller to report whether he considers that he has any officer in the Munster District Capable of Capturing them: if so Major Miller will order him to the district forthwith: He will put under his Command such Additional force as he may require and he will furnish him with any individual policeman whom he may point out as likely from their intrepidy and sagacity to assist him in his duty.[23]

Major Miller chose Chief Constable Carroll, 'the most experienced Policeman in Munster', for the task.[24] Carroll was recalled from Cahirciveen, County Kerry, briefed in Cork by Miller and was in County Waterford by 28 December 1835. Success for Carroll would 'constitute a strong claim to his Excellency's favourable consideration'.[25]

As if not stretched enough by the Connerys, the County Waterford Constabulary had to contend with 'the most daring gang of robbers that has appeared in the County for many years against whose attacks bolts, bars, & Watchmen are of no avail'.[26] On the night of 4 December 1835, an armed gang broke into the offices of the Mining Company of Ireland at Knockmahon, overpowered the watchman, smashed the safe with sledge hammers and escaped with the payroll. Their haul included £100 in silver and £580 in £1 and £1 10s 0d denomination notes of the Bank of Ireland. The Mining Company acted immediately, stopped payment on the notes and circularised posters bearing dates and serial numbers, warning the public not to accept them in payment.[27]

Although Sylvanus Jones R.M. and Mathew Singleton R.M., Carrick-on-Suir held an immediate inquiry, in which some of the watchmen, who came under suspicion for compliance with the raiders, were interviewed, the police made little progress. Chief Constable Lumsden of Tramore provided the intriguing information that a man called Walsh, recently dismissed from the copper mine for bad conduct and who was connected with the Connerys, was suspected of being implicated.[28] It may have been that the Connerys had had some tenuous link with the operation: the precise planning and execution could reflect the influence of John Connery.

A father and son, James and John Casey of Carrickbeg, were arrested within a month of each other for passing cancelled notes and were sentenced to seven years transportation at the County Waterford Spring Assizes of 1836. The principals in the robbery still remained at large. In a bizarre twist John Casey put a proposal to Mathew Singleton, R.M. acting in the hope that the Mining Company of Ireland would intercede for pardon he would require the raiders to return the proceeds of the robbery; should they fail he would name them. The robbers had resorted to altering serial numbers and getting others to pass them off, in an attempt to liquidate the Bank of Ireland notes. When a month had passed without result, Richard Purdey, the Secretary of the Mining Company, requested Thomas Drummond to remove the Caseys to the hulks to concentrate John's mind.[29] This could not be implemented immediately in John's case, as he had escaped with the Connerys on 22 May 1836.

On recapture he told Singleton he could no longer deliver on any part of his proposal. He said that the raid had been carried out by a five man gang with inside help from a watchman. He named two of the raiders as Thomas Sullivan and Gough, now conveniently resident in America, but said that the remainder were unknown to him. He was by now, a man 'anxious to be transported'.[30] Significantly, John Casey was with John and Patrick Connery when he was recaptured. The police never caught the Knockmahon raiders.

In a letter to Lord Morpeth on 23 December 1835, Major Miller perceived the continued failure to capture the Connerys as symptomatic of Irish popular attitudes to law and order:

> That these Felons – continually hunted, as I have reason to believe, by the Police should still roam at large, is attributable to the facilities afforded them, in the part of the Country which they infest, of betaking themselves to extensive tract of Mountain remote from the Stations of the Constabulary, & still more to the feelings of the Peasantry whose sympathies are always with the Criminal, whom they harbour & succour although his misdeeds, perhaps are abhorrent to them. In most civilized Countries, the Officers of Justice are encouraged and assisted in their pursuit of offenders. In Ireland, they are baffled and obstructed: And, such is the infamy attached to the mere name of Informer & such vengeance with which those suspected even of giving information are too frequently visited & the very outrage in question [the attack on Sylvester Greaney] is an

instance of the sort – that the most revolting Crimes pass unpunished because those who could assist in making the Perpetrators amenable to the Laws are deterred, by fears or prejudices, from doing their duty to the Community.[31]

Meanwhile, Sub-Inspector Samuel Croker had a limited success to report. On Christmas Day 1835, a search of the orchard of William Connery near Aglish, yielded a short gun loaded with slugs, bearing John Connery's name cut into the stock. The gun was in an old hut, some distance from the house, used for watching the orchard in summertime. Croker was convinced that John was close by:

it appears that he left it behind on the approach of the Police, I am certain that he was at that moment lying concealed in some ditch or brake near the place, but although the Police redoubled their exertions, and made the most diligent search we could not discover him, you may be assured if I could have got the most distant view of him I would have him alive or dead.[32]

In what was to become a familiar pattern, William Connery was unaware that the Connerys were there and denied assisting them. He admitted that they had called to his house a few days before the search and that John had a gun, but they were just passing through. The Police were unimpressed and sought to have William Connery convicted for possession of an unregistered firearm, since he had no licence to keep arms. The magistrates, sitting at Villierstown Petty Sessions, referred the matter to the Chief Law Officer in the Chief Secretary's Office, Maziere Brady, for his opinion. Brady advised that Connery would not be properly convicted in this instance.[33]

Despite the gun episode, the overall security situation was bleak. The Connerys found ideal cover in 'the great extent of wild and thickly wooded country', provided by the Colligan river valley, the Comeragh-Monavullagh uplands and the dense wooded glens of the Blackwater and its tributaries.[34] Croker estimated their popular support to be such that the houses in which they stayed were always watched by people on guard and that there was surveillance of the police stations. Moreover the government reward had as yet produced no information. With such widespread obstruction he felt it imperative for Chief Constable Carroll to arrive disguised.

In late January 1836 Croker was laid low by an attack of nervous exhaustion. This had been brought on by the mental strain and prolonged exposure to the elements which the pursuit of the Connerys had entailed. Nevertheless, he secured lodging for Carroll and two other men in the house of Patrick Morrissey, a farmer of Whitechurch.[35] The success with which this was kept secret is illustrated by a notice which appeared at Ballinameela Chapel on Sunday 24 January 1836.

Patrick Morrissey

Take notice this day that Your Keeping police in Your House for the purpose of Hunting the Connerys – any person or persons would duo Sow would Surely take the Rewarde if Your not able to pay Rent without Keeping police Give up your land to the devil – Let every person and persons take notice this day if Mr. Morrissey the Gentlemon Gives any More Lodgings to police that he will Surely Suffer for it police Must Keep their Regular barriks. Mr. Morrissey this is the first and last notice be Sure or Sorry

January 24th 1836.[36]

The Connerys were extending their psychological warfare to the management of the police pursuit. On the following Sunday, in the same chapel, the extent of the Connerys' popular support was highlighted. Fr. Michael O'Connor C.C., Aglish and Ballinameela, skilled preacher in Irish and Tithe activist, addressed the congregation on the subject of inconsistencies of the police in relation to crime. He is reported to have said that the police were very active in the area of keeping forcible possession in contrast to their conduct on petty robberies. According to Sub-Constable Henry Burke, Cappagh, he then proceeded to question the necessity for such a selective police force, 'that the Farmers of the countery need not be supporting the peelers if they like that they could keepe down these Robers if they like'.[37] The congregation needed little convincing of the social parasitism of the police, 'the People in the Chapple sait it was a pity to give the peelers any thing to eat and that it was a pity but to choak them'.[38]

This indirect, clerical sanction offered Croker and Miller a means of explaining their lack of progress against the Connerys; 'the success of the Connerys in eluding the Police need not cause surprise when a Clergyman having influence with the People thus interposes on their behalf'.[39]

Presumbably it also provided a basis, around which a theory of clerical conspiracy could be developed. The Carrick-on-Suir correspondent of the ultra-reactionary *Tipperary Constitution* titillated his readership with the following sensational disclosure:

There are some Rev. R.C. Clergymen, at the bottom of this subject, who countenanced, abetted and sheltered the Connerys, whose names and motives for so doing will shortly appear before the public.[40]

In the end, however, fear of the law of libel appears to have cooled his investigative ardour and the names were not published. The clergy of Waterford and Lismore was very different from the vulnerable body they had been in the time of Fr. Nicholas Sheehy. Then, Whiteboyism had provided a convenient excuse for a cull of the minor Catholic gentry of South Tipperary by the frightened local Ascendancy.[41] Thus, accusations of support for the Connerys could do little to check the clergy's newly gained political power. In the event, the Connerys soon demonstrated publicly, in a manner which precluded police excuses, what a formidable proposition they presented as individuals.

The Police finally caught up with the Connerys on the evening of 13 February 1836. Chief Constable Francis Crossley of Dungarvan, 'a brave, enterprising and intelligent officer',[42] received information that the Connerys, their sister and others were drinking in a field within a mile of town. He sent six of his men to Colligan turnpike to block the Connerys' line of retreat towards Bohadoon and the mountains. Then, he set off with the remaining five, and came upon the Connerys (brothers and sister) and a companion sitting on a ditch at Ballinamuck Cross, a quarter of a mile from town. The Connerys took to the fields, ignoring Crossley's threats to open fire on them if they did not stand. Whereupon Crossley ordered three of his men to fire on them and a gun battle began. The Connerys replied with a blunderbuss loaded with slugs and heavy shot, which came near to finding its mark: 'we narrowly escaped, as it passed over our heads'.[43]

The police fired two more shots and the Connerys returned fire once before escaping in the darkness. Although one of the policemen saw one of the Connerys fall, a search of the area next morning by Crossley revealed no traces of blood.

Crossley's intelligence information stated that the Connerys had decided to go to America and were raising funds among the farmers for that purpose. In his report to Major Miller, he wanted persons who knew the Connerys sent to the ports of Cove, Youghal and Limerick. He also advised that the government proclamation, with its £50 reward, be renewed.

Thomas Drummond's action on this information was thorough and complete. He had the proclamation renewed for a further six months and descriptions of the Connerys inserted in the *Hue and Cry*. He ordered that copies of the proclamation be dispatched to the police authorities and emigration agents at the ports of Cove, Youghal, Waterford, Limerick and Dublin, and to the trans-shipment centres of Liverpool and Bristol.[44]

America would not be easily attained by the Connerys. The business of securing a passage involved risky meetings with emigration agents which, when combined with the need to wait for the ship to sail would have greatly increased the probability of detection. In order to leave Ireland the Connerys would have to come to the authorities.

Those authorities' efforts as personified by Chief Constable Carroll continued as before. Though 'almost dead from the work he had done', Carroll had little success.[45] An informant called Hurley had promised to set the Connerys for him on 12 February 1836. In the time-honoured tradition of Irish hospitality, Hurley had invited the Connerys to dine with him in order to betray them. However, the Connerys were not so easily entrapped. A joint search of Ballylemon Wood by Crossley, Sylvanus Jones R.M. and Carroll proved fruitless. According to Carroll, the Connerys had received funds from several of the gentry in the neighbourhood – presumably to facilitate their speedy emigration.[46] Indeed, there is a strong suspicion that Thomas Foley made some financial settlement with the Connerys. Despite the police failures, Dublin Castle had received no representations from him since early November 1835. Moreover, the Connerys' escape from gaol in May 1836 evoked no response from Foley. It may be that Foley's silence points to the existence of a secret payment to the Connerys, in good faith and without determination of liability.

Police intelligence about Connery emigration plans was soon confirmed. It appears that Patrick and John arrived in Waterford city on the evening of 6 March 1836 to book passages for America.[47] They took lodgings in the house of Patrick Connors, publican and tailor, of Barrack Street. However, Patrick McGrath, a tailor in Connors's employment, saw his opportunity and reported their presence to James Bruce, the Governor of the County Gaol. On 7 March 1836 a military detachment surrounded the house and, in a co-ordinated operation, Bruce and George Wright, High Constable of the city, arrested both brothers in an upstairs room. Although the Connerys possessed both a sword and pistol, with quantities of heavy shot and gunpowder they bowed to the overwhelming force. As they were being removed one of them remarked in Irish to his uncle, 'What a damnable place you have brought us to'.[48]

McGrath, in the meantime, was becoming afraid of reprisals. Moreover, his treachery meant no one around Waterford would employ him. He enlisted the aid of Henry Winston Barron M.P. for Waterford and some of the city magistrates to get him a job in the police or another safe and distant government sinecure on what he considered were the eminent grounds:

Your Memorialist respectfully begs to state that he has always maintained an honest and upright character through life and that his motive for giving the Information above alluded to were to rid the Country of such Pests of Society, and is now in danger of losing his life by remaining in this part of the United Kingdom.[49]

The response of Thomas Drummond, transmitted via Major Miller was chilly. McGrath possessed neither the minimum height or character for the police, 'Mr. Drummond is of the opinion that it is by no means expedient to provide for Informers by giving them appointments in the Police.'[50]

Furthermore since McGrath had collected all the rewards (£100) it was considered that he had been adequately compensated.[51] Despite outlining the official position in the matter Miller would of course place the case before the government if Barron so wished. Drummond's position remained consistent. Despite further correspondence from Barron it is presumed that McGrath had to fend for himself.[52]

Patrick Connors, the publican, was similarly concerned with harmful public opinion. The *Waterford Mail* had named him as the man who told Bruce where the Connerys were. In a letter published in the *Chronicle* and *Mail* he denied any connection with the arrest of the Connerys and stated that he was losing business because people were putting around such tales and he wanted a stop put to them.[53]

If James Bruce's high profile in the recapture of the Connerys had been providential for his reputation, the publication of the deposition of John Connery in the *Mail* of 9 March 1836 appeared to exonerate Bruce of any involvement in the Connerys' escape from the Clogheen bridewell. John Connery deposed to Michael Power Ronayne J.P. that he and Patrick had broken the bolts on their irons in the bridewell kitchen. He said that Jackson, the bridewell keeper, had given them whiskey and becoming drunk, had taken them into the yard two or three times and had even offered to take off their bolts. It was only when Jackson pointed out the path of a previous escape that they decided to attempt one. The motives of the Connerys' bizarre intervention appears to have been the need to conciliate Bruce, to ensure that the conditions of their confinement would not preclude another escape attempt. On another level, the Connerys' world would be impressed and appreciative of the comical irony of convicts pronouncing on a gaoler.

Such appeasement of Bruce was timely for he faced the charge of wilfully and negligently permitting the escape from his custody of Patrick and John at Clogheen bridewell, at the Tipperary Spring Assizes, held at Clonmel on 15 March 1836. The Crown sought a postponement to prepare its evidence for the next assizes. Bound in his own recognizance of £100 to appear at the Summer Assizes Bruce succeeded in getting another postponement.[54] The Crown prosecution appears to have been taken no further as by then events appeared to have rendered it superfluous. James Bruce had been dismissed as Governor of the County Gaol and acquitted on similar charges concerning the great Connery escape at the County Waterford Summer Assizes.

It was in terms of triumph tinged with relief that Thomas Drummond was able to inform the Attorney-General, Michael O'Loghlen, on 8 March 1836, 'Caught at last!'.[55]

The Irish Administration now had one less problem to deal with. Chief Constable Carroll was able to leave County Waterford to take up charge of the Nenagh district. All that remained was to decide whether the public good would be better served by the instant transportation of the Connerys or by a new trial of the brothers for their escape and various offences committed while on the run. Such Crown options became irrelevant when

John and Patrick led another successful jailbreak from the County Gaol on 22 May 1836. Thomas Drummond's elation had been premature.

This escape was an extremely well thought-out and executed operation. It involved a fortnight's meticulous planning and even the development of an alternate escape route. The financial and logistical impetus to begin planning was apparently provided by a visit to the Connerys by their sister. It appears likely also that a James Connery, coach driver, on the Cork and Waterford mail, who was dismissed from his position with the Post Office because of his conduct during the escape may have been the Connerys' uncle.[56]

At seven o'clock on Sunday evening, 22 May 1836, a turnkey called James McLaughlin was asked for water by one of the prisoners. When he opened the door, to pass the bucket, he was overpowered and a jacket placed over his head by one of the Connerys. The prisoners recovered a key from him and freed their comrades in an adjoining downstairs room – not all of whom wished to escape. A group of fourteen men, led by the Connerys, rushed down into the inner (treadmill) yard. John Connery used the treadmill weight to smash the lock on the yard door. Some of the prisoners had gained the outer yard when the alarm was raised, but James Bruce attempted to stop the rest. He was knocked over and the prisoners smashed the lock on the door of the outer yard to secure their freedom. The whole escape took about nine minutes.[57] The fourteen armed themselves with stones but Ballybricken (city district) gave them a tumultuous welcome: shouting, 'don't stop us!', the Connerys were cheered along the Cork Road.[58] When they had reached the city bounds one of the Connerys addressed the crowd and told them to disperse so as the police would not get them. As the escapees dispersed they exhorted the people: 'if they saw soldiers and police coming after them, to send them in another direction'.[59]

At the subsequent inquiry presided over by Major B. Woodward, Inspector General of Prisons in Ireland, James Bruce's administration of the County Gaol was rudely exposed. Woodward reported to Thomas Drummond, 'The Governor is an old and infirm man who was never possessed of a capacity suited to so important a trust'.[60] Each watchman had a blunderbuss but the powder was not kept beside it. In the midst of the escape only Bruce was able to procure an unprimed and useless blunderbuss. One of the watchmen, James McLaughlin had gone missing during the fateful events. Woodward also found the prison architecture severely deficient and recommended structural repairs to make it secure. Bruce paid the full penalty; he was dismissed as Governor and, together with James McLaughlin faced serious charges at the County Summer Assizes.

Early on the morning of 25 May 1836, a detachment of the Cappoquin police under Constable Major Atkins, came on three men in a field, they ran and were fired on. John Casey, was hit in the heel but John and Patrick Connery escaped in the darkness:

> John, who is an expert swimmer dashed thro' the river Blackwater and laughed at those who had not the courage or ability to follow him, whilst Patrick not being acquainted with the watery element, took advantage of his brother's retreat across the river, and hid himself in the copsewood and briars at the side ...[61]

While Casey was lodged in Dungarvan gaol, awaiting his return to Waterford, a relative of the Connerys visited him and let slip that Patrick had been slightly wounded in the side when the police opened fire. This coincided with a rumour that the Connerys were despairing of retaining their freedom and were about to surrender.[62] Later events, however, suggest that the Connerys were once again manipulating public opinion.

Dublin Castle offered rewards of £30 a head for the recapture of the fourteen. John Casey was joined by Edmond Murphy, who was under sentence of transportation for sheep stealing and had been captured in his own home at Clashmore. By 31 May 1836 Denis Mahony, on remand for larceny, had also been retaken. On 28 June 1836 Sylvanus Jones R.M. could report the capture of John Daniel, who was under sentence of transportation for seven years for violent assault. With the recapture of James Leonard, under sentence of transportation for seven years for pig stealing, by the Ardfinnan police and John Capless, a goat-stealing offender, in the west of County Waterford; only eight prisoners remained at large by 11 July 1836. The Connerys remained elusive, their pursuit hampered by the deficiencies in police intelligence which have been remarked on before. Between 24 May and 26 July 1836 Chief Constable Crossley had two persons employed in gaining information about the Connerys' movements.[63] The benefits of such covert surveillance were immediately outweighed by Crossley's seemingly fortuitous interception of a letter from Liverpool.

> On another occasion, John succeeded in transmitting a letter to Liverpool by a friend, stating that he was about to take his departure to America. The letter was addressed to his father, who with his two sisters, now reside in Dungarvan, posted in the Liverpool post office, and written with such skill as to deceive the acutest. It reached Dungarvan. The father made no secret of its contents. Word immediately went to the police that such a document had been received.[64]

Thomas Drummond reacted swiftly and ordered Crossley to proceed to Liverpool directly. One week after the letter had been posted, Francis Crossley arrived in Liverpool. His luck appeared to hold as he found that a westerly gale had ensured that only two boats had sailed since the letter had been posted on 11 July. He found no trace of the Connerys' names on the agents' books but it was expected the bad weather would force the ships back to port. Once the wind abated a little, it was Crossley's intention to search all the vessels in port: 'I am partly certain they are on board one of these Vessels'.[65] Such was Crossley's optimism that his only problem concerned money. He was afraid he would not have sufficient to bring the Connerys back to Ireland if he captured them. Thomas Drummond sent him £20. Francis Crossley did not find the Connerys in Liverpool. According to the sensational 'Interesting Particulars of their Extraordinary Escapes and Adventures':

> this simple but brilliantly executed Connery deception achieved its total objective. They had successfully convinced their pursuers that they had escaped to America and dispatches were sent to the various police stations on the look out for them, that there was no occasion to trouble themselves for the future as the Connerys were not in the country. The Connerys were now in the possession of almost perfect liberty.[66]

The paucity of official correspondence from August 1836 onwards suggests a large scaling down of the search for the Connerys. A relaxation of the search in County Waterford, qualified by continued surveillance at the ports (it had been widened to include Belfast and Londonderry), would have allowed Thomas Drummond to redeploy police resources while still maintaining adequate cover should the Connerys reappear. The Connerys' behaviour following their escape allowed Drummond new room to manoeuvre. In contrast to their previous violent stage, they no longer constituted an armed threat. Moreover, neither Thomas Foley or anyone else felt sufficiently in danger from them to write to Dublin Castle. Furthermore, the government proclamation offering £30 rewards did not expire until November 1836.

While the Connerys' tactical brilliance gained them some respite, the leaving of Ireland with its successful negotiation of the ports continued as dangerous as ever. Notoriety imposed its own powerful constraints. The Connerys found themselves unable to duplicate what they had simulated. It is indicative of their frustration and lack of progress that they dropped all pretence of having escaped to America, in order to exploit political developments. They perceived the death of King William IV and the accession of Victoria as synonymous with the extension of the royal prerogative of mercy, which traditionally marked a new reign. Patrick Smith of Lisarow, Dungarvan, prominent in local politics, wrote to Thomas Drummond, on their behalf, seeking permission for the Connerys to emigrate to the United States or the British Colonies. The advice of the Lord Lieutenant was that unconditional surrender only would be accepted.[67] Smith's reaction was extremely diplomatic:

I am satisfied they will surrender if I advise them to do so but I feel the utmost delicacy and in fact embarrassment under the circumstances to take the responsibility of giving such advice.[68]

Meanwhile Thomas Drummond exploited the Connerys' formal reappearance by having the house of Patrick Smith watched. He planned that when they arrived to learn the fate of Smith's proposal the police would capture them. Sub-Inspector Samuel Croker also held out high hopes of a person who sought a job in the police for his brother and to whom Croker had offered £50 for each of the Connerys.[69] Patrick and John did not fall into this trap, however. Despite this rebuff they continued to pursue hopes of a political solution. This time the brothers attempted to enlist the aid of the highest political level accessible to them.

On 21 October 1837, they sought the help of Henry Villiers Stuart of Dromana, Lord Lieutenant of the County, to intercede with the government, on their behalf to secure a pardon. The hero of 1826 had retained his political popularity while combining it with influence within the Whig Government. He was created Lord Stuart de Decies on 10 May 1839. Daniel O'Connell saw him as an ideal leader who epitomised what the majority of his class unfortunately were not:

> The great evil of Ireland is the estrangement between the people of the class who belong, or claim to belong, to the aristocratic and landed gentry. The far greater part of that class entertain an envenomed hatred of the Irish people.[70]

Villiers Stuart did not offer the Connerys anything, rather he reinforced the position of Dublin Castle:

> I immediately enquired whether they were prepared to surrender themselves unconditionally into custody and upon them returning an evasive answer, I dispatched my servant to Villierstown for a Party of the Police.[71]

As Villierstown was two miles away the Connerys had an hour's start before the police arrived which they put to good effect. With their negotiation strategy now a failure, the Connerys were confronted with the depressing reality of what to do next.

The inquiry into the great Connery escape had its sequel at the County Waterford Summer Assizes on 12 July 1836. James Bruce, the ex-gaoler, was indicted for having wilfully and negligently permitted and suffered John Connery and Patrick Connery, two convicted felons, to escape from his custody. Bruce was defended by William H. Hassard and was able to present the Church of Ireland chaplain, a member of the Board of Superintendence of the Gaol and a former sub-sheriff, to speak on his behalf. The jury was out for two to three minutes and returned a verdict of not guilty.[72]

James McLaughlin, the watchman, was not so lucky: he was convicted

41

of knowingly and wilfully assisting the prisoners in their escape. One of his colleagues testified how 'the prisoners had been tampering with him and offering him some money three weeks previous to the escape'.[73] McLaughlin bore the brunt of the responsibility and was sentenced to seven years transportation by Chief Justice Doherty.

James Bruce proved irrepressible amid his misfortune. He brazenly attempted to capitalise on his acquittal and secure compensation for loss of employment and pension. His memorial to Lord Mulgrave, the Lord Lieutenant, of 9 August 1836 had no less than eighty two signatures of dignitaries affixed but Thomas Drummond was not amused:

> His Excellency has no power to grant such compensation, and if he had, he would certainly not give it to a Governor of a Gaol under whose negligent charge much mischief has occured.[74]

Although the Connerys could not be found their faction the Poleens continued to trouble the authorities. Chief Constable Crossley had just returned from Liverpool, when at the fair of Whitechurch, on 5 August 1836, he was confronted with the most serious outbreak of Poleen/Gow violence of the whole decade. What began as an ordinary faction riot escalated into a deliberately planned attack on the military and police. The Riot Act was read by Sylvanus Jones R.M. and the police came very close to opening fire. Thomas Drummond took a serious view of the Whitechurch affair and a cavalry unit was dispatched to Dungarvan to prevent any repetition.[75] Whitechurch was to prove the high water mark of Poleen/Gow violence at fairs.

The Melbourne Administration in Ireland from its very beginnings had concerned itself with suppressing breaches of the peace, whether occasioned by fairs, party meetings or Orange Parades. Thomas Drummond was able to explain, to the Select Committee of the House of Lords on Crime in Ireland in 1839, how specific measures introduced to deal with faction fights in late 1835 and early 1836 were consolidated into a general order to constabulary of June 1836. It began with a policy statement and then detailed the correct procedure to be followed by the constabulary: 'It is the determination of the Lord Lieutenant that every exertion shall be made to suppress party and faction fights at fairs, markets, or any other occasion'.[76]

For Drummond, the authorities determination as embodied in this regulation together with the Spirit Licence Act of 1836, which allowed a magistrate to order an end to the sale of liquor as well as to clear the fair booths had brought the faction problem under control:

> The certainty that persons engaged in such riots would be brought to justice, and the fact of the leaders having been apprehended, on some occasions previous to an intended disturbance, and in others on the spot, have had the effect, I think, of putting down these outrages.[77]

Sylvanus Jones was able to tell the same Select Committee, somewhat immodestly, how such measures, in particular the strong authority presence at fairs and night police patrols, had subdued the County Waterford Factions:

> A new State of Things arose, and the People, having Confidence in the Protection afforded by the Presence of the Military and Police under my direction at Fairs, returned to the Fairs, and Business at Fairs went on as usual. Confidence was restored both at the Fairs and in returning from Fairs by Patrols.[78]

Certainly the scale of Poleen/Gow violence at fairs declined drastically from the halcyon levels of 1833-4, but the other facet of the feud, the isolated attack still remained difficult to pre-empt and the continuation of these though reduced in number testified to the resilience of the factions. However, increasingly effective pressure on the Connery *demi-monde* boded ill for the brothers' future.

In general, the popular support engendered by the Connerys tended to be passive in nature, but on occasion it did take concrete form. On the night of 15 August 1836, Richard and Michael Whelan went to Redmond Bransfield's house in Lackinsilla, looking for Thomas Connell. When they discovered 'the informer's son' in bed, Richard Whelan 'beat him in an unmerciful manner with a loaded whip on the naked body'.[79] Sub-Inspector Samuel Croker later learned from young Connell that he attributed the motive for this assault to the suspicion that his father had given information to the police about the Connerys. Whether Thomas Connell was one of Chief Constable Crossley's employees is unclear, but it is worth noting that Patrick Connery escaped through a back window in Bransfields', in late September 1835, when pursued by the police. It is likely that Bransfields was a safe house for the Connerys and when there were leakages of information to the police, suspicion fell on others who congregated there, like the Connells. Croker took information against the Whelans, but there was no attempt by the authorities to see young Connell's punishment as other than retrospective and to question seriously the Connerys' supposed emigration.

Unlike the Connerys, the strain of evading the authorities proved too great for some. One of the escapees, Michael Dower, under sentence of transportation for life for manslaughter, surrendered to Sylvanus Jones R.M. at Dungarvan in early October 1836.

Shortly afterwards, the fruits of the Lord Lieutenant's inquiry into the Irish convict service were felt when the hulks, *Surprise* at Cove and *Essex* at Kingstown, were abolished.

Kilmainham Gaol became the central convict depot from which convicts were to be conveyed to the transports for immediate transportation. In 1839 Thomas Drummond was able to report to the Select Committee of the House of Lords on Crime that the new system combined prison reform with financial rectitude. The Lord Lieutenant's inquiry had found the long period spent on board the hulks by prisoners to be 'a very injurious system'; that the hulks as prisons were, 'most imperfect' and 'did not admit of that attention to classification which a prison on shore allows'.[80] The abolition of the hulks resulted, by implication, in a more humane, efficient Irish convict service, at the same time reducing costs by almost £8000 per annum.

The *Waterford Chronicle* reflected the appeal which this measure had for the liberal middle class; it would now take only one night to travel to Kilmainham by coach, at one eighth the cost of the former three day journey to Cork, with a large escort.[81] For the Connerys capture now meant no more Clogheen interludes.

The paper's reaction to another proposed innovation in the administration of justice – the removal of the County Assizes to Dungarvan – was very different. In November 1834, a meeting in Dungarvan Courthouse, had precipitated the controversy when a memorial was forwarded to the Lord Lieutenant, seeking the removal of the County Assizes to Dungarvan, because of that town's central location. This request had the support of all the major West Waterford gentry, including John Mathew Galwey M.P., Sir Richard Keane M.P., Henry and William Villiers Stuart and Pierce George Barron.[82] The effect was to produce instant political consensus in East Waterford and the city: Henry Winston Barron and William Christmas (Tory), normally opponents, were equally vociferous in their condemnation of Western Particularism.[83] Defenders of the status quo insisted that a burden of £50,000 would be put on the county cess (rates) if the assizes were to be moved because of the need to construct a County Gaol and Courthouse in Dungarvan.[84] A letter written to the *Waterford Mail* invoked the ability of the Poleens and Gows to pervert the course of justice in the event of such a move:

> What a pretty question it was to bring before the Judges! To bring them to Dungarvan amongst a tribe of ferocious savages in the persons of the Poleens and Gows – the people of the town themselves are quiet and respectable, but the crowds of fellows that live in the wilds – who would be safe within their reach? No, Dungarvan must become a little more civilized before it can compete with the metropolis of the county.[85]

Meetings were convened all over the county in an effort to show how unrepresentative the Dungarvan partisans were.

At a hearing on the matter, which the Irish Privy Council held in May 1837, Thomas Foley of Tourtane, Lismore appeared as a witness for the removal, citing the inconvenience of Waterford city for the inhabitants of the county. Sir Richard Keane was also examined. John Keane, an architect, produced costings which put a new Dungarvan Gaol at £25,000 against £14,000 for improvements to the existing County Gaol. He also calculated that a new courthouse in Dungarvan would cost £10,000 which was less than that of replacing the existing city courthouse. Dr. Robert Keane, chemist, testified to the purity of the Dungarvan water supply which was four times more improving than the water in Waterford. When Major James Palmer was questioned about his recent inspection of the County Gaol, he conceded that, even with improvements, he 'could not make it an effective building'.[86] Thus, indirectly, the Connerys' escape had underlined the vulnerability of the gaol and appeared to support the case put forward for the removal of the assizes.

Despite the careful Western presentation their proposal was not to succeed. Thus 'this monstrous scheme by which a few gentlemen of the West and some 20 to 30 Dungarvan shopkeepers hoped to saddle their county with an enormous intolerable taxation to gratify their own cupidity', lost out to metropolitan self-interest presented, as it was, as the purest, disinterested concern.[87] The removal of the County Assizes threatened a translation of political and economic status to Dungarvan, an insidious decapitalisation of the city.

Another of the fourteen, Robert Browne who had been in custody for assault, was recaptured, and convicted at the County Spring Assizes for 1837 of escaping from the County Gaol. Edmond Power, who had been in custody for attacking a farmer's house, was similarly convicted at the following Summer Assizes.

Indeed, when Constable Sides arrested two men at Killinick, County Wexford on 12 April 1837 he thought he had captured John Connery. However, when Thomas Drummond was informed that 'They both appear to be very simple and are in a miserable state', he was extremely sceptical, 'but I think A [as above] cannot be applicable to either of the Connerys'.[88] It later transpired that one of the men had burned a house in Longford and his companion – whom Sides had thought was John Connery – was later held on a vagrancy charge.

In the early morning of 19 December 1837, Chief Constable George Wright and the city police raided the house of a farmer called Spense at Killure, about three miles from Waterford, and recaptured another escapee – Thomas Kinneally. Kinneally had been in custody on a perjury charge, but he was now working as a servant for Spense.[89] The police were accompanied by their informant Patrick Dillon, a Kilmacthomas tailor, who had led them to believe that they would take the Connerys as well. Despite this partial success Dillon was bitterly disappointed. He complained to his handler Chief Constable Edward Ashbury of Kilmacthomas that he had not received the £30 reward for the recapture of Kinneally.[90] In early December a disgruntled Dillon made a sensational offer to Ashbury – he would set the Connerys if he got his £30 for Kinneally. Little was done to placate the frustrated informer. Major Miller, now Deputy Inspector General of Constabulary, maintained that Dillon had received the reward for Kinneally. The emphasis was placed on the Connerys and Ashbury was to be advised to ascertain whether two could be had for the price of one:

> Inform Chief Constable Ashbury that £30 – the sum Dillon obtained for the arrest of Kinneally will be paid for the apprehension of each of Connerys but it may be well that Mr. Ashbury should ascertain before he makes the above communication – whether Dillons own proposition is not to the effect that he will set both for thirty pounds.[91]

The Connerys' meeting with Henry Villiers Stuart had produced prompt action on the part of Chief Constable Francis Crossley. On his advice, the government reward was renewed on 26 October 1837, proclamations were sent to County Waterford, and police strength at Villierstown was increased. Crossley had recommended that the reward be increased and insisted that it be renewed, at the very least:

> as the persons who were after them in 1836 think the Reward is out of date and if they get them they would not be paid for their trouble and risk ...[92]

For Crossley the situation was now fully clarified 'as there can now be no doubt of these men having returned to the Country ...'.[93]

On 13 January Acting Sub-Inspector Crossley received a complaint from John Hearn, an Aglish publican, that John Connery had seriously assaulted him on the night of 10 January 1838. Hearn said that he and two others were returning home from Dungarvan at eleven o'clock. They called in to William Brown's public house at Ballinameela, where they were joined by John Connery. All were refused whiskey, so the party went on to John Kelly's and drank some spirits there. When they left, John Connery took a bottle of whiskey with him, which he shared with his companions. When they reached Woodstock, John Connery accused Hearn of refusing him drink in the past and complained that he had been blamed for the fate of the Collinses.[94] Hearn replied, 'no John you were not ...'.[95] According to Hearn, John Connery pulled him down, kicked him in the side, breaking four or five ribs and injuring his thigh. He believed that he would have been murdered were it not for his companions' intervention. He attributed his delay in reporting the incident to 'fear and dread to say anything about or against the "Conneris"'.[96] Crossley believed that the same fear was inhibiting the farmers of the County from giving the vital information which would lead to their arrest. He felt that the reward would have to be increased in order to outweigh those fears:

if some strong inducement is not held out to those who would give

No. 12,879.

[861]

The Dublin Gazette.

Published by Authority.

FRIDAY, OCTOBER 27, 1837.

DUBLIN CASTLE,
October 23, 1837.

HIS Excellency the Lord Lieutenant has been pleased to appoint John Mason Pooley, Esq., to be Comptroller of His Excellency's Household, vice Stewart, who resigns. Appointment to bear date 1st October, 1837.

DUBLIN CASTLE,
October 25, 1837.

WHEREAS it has been represented to the Lord Lieutenant, that on the Night of the 21st instant, as John Wall and Michael Querny were returning from the Town of Mountrath, accompanied by their Wives, to their Residence, Boherard, Parish of Aghavoe, in the Queen's County, Three Men came from behind a Ditch, at Clonard, and struck Querny with a Stone, from the Effects of which he immediately expired :

His Excellency, for the better apprehending and bringing to Justice the Perpetrators of this Murder, is pleased hereby to offer a Reward of

FIFTY POUNDS

to any Person or Persons (except the Person or Persons who actually committed the same,) who shall, within Six Months from the date hereof, give such Information as shall lead to the apprehension and conviction of all or any of the Persons concerned therein.

By His Excellency's Command,
MORPETH.

DUBLIN CASTLE,
October 26, 1837.

WHEREAS it has been represented to the Lord Lieutenant, that on the 22d May, 1836, Patrick and John Connery escaped from the Gaol of Waterford, while under sentence of Transportation :

His Excellency, for the better apprehending and bringing to Justice the above named Individuals, is pleased hereby to offer a Reward of

THIRTY POUNDS

to any Person or Persons who shall, within Six Months from the date hereof, give such Information as shall lead to their apprehension.

By His Excellency's Command,
MORPETH.

Description of Patrick Connery—aged about 38 years ; height about 6 feet ; round shouldered, and stoops, brown hair, sharp visage, little or no whiskers, very thin beard, aquiline nose, sharp chin, nose and face a little scorbutic, countenance otherwise pale; speaks English very imperfectly ; a thin athletic man ; and a native of the County of Waterford.

John Connery—aged from 28 to 30 years ; about 5 feet 10 inches in height ; brown hair, light active figure, small dark whiskers, fair complexion, well looking, square shouldered, and upright in his carriage ; speaks English well ; and a native of the County of Waterford.

From the LONDON GAZETTE of Tuesday, October 24, 1837.

St. James's-Palace, September 22, 1837.

THE Queen has been pleased, on the nomination of Lord Foley, to appoint James Bunce Curling, Esq. one of Her Majesty's Honourable Corps of Gentlemen at Arms, vice Harrison.

Dublin Gazette Reward Notice, 27 Oct. 1837.

information, it will be impossible to take them, every Stratagem has been resorted to, but I am sorry to say without Succeeding...[97]

Crossley received authorisation to offer £50 for such private information. The Connerys became lucrative again.

The attack on Hearn marked the first recorded misdemeanour committed by either of the Connerys since their great escape. John Connery's reported concern about the public perception of his role in the Collins' affair suggests he was worried about a shift in popular opinion. John's reaction was, no doubt due to frustration and a nagging fear that repudiation by the community, which had sealed the fate of the raparees in the past, awaited the Connerys.

On this occasion the restraining presence of Patrick Connery was absent – he may have been confined to bed with fever. The irrepressible Dillon had renewed his offer to Chief Constable Ashbury:

he has two Conneries (sic) Set, and will accompany me to the place if he gets the reward that he was entitled to for the arrest of Kinneally, otherwise he will not discover them.[98]

Dillon had made two suits of clothes for the Connerys and was able to tell Ashbury that one of the brothers was very ill from fever. Even though Ashbury felt sure Dillon would betray the Connerys if the outstanding Kinneally matter was settled, Dublin Castle declined to address that aspect of the impasse. Thomas Drummond wrote, 'This sum viz. £30 will be given to him if he performs the service'.[99] It is unclear why Dublin Castle made no attempt to conciliate Dillon, while it is likely that the £30 reward for Kinneally lapsed in November 1836 with others of the fourteen still at liberty – no attempt was made to make an extraordinary payment to him as a gesture of good will. The easiest way to alienate an informer was to treat his actions as those of an unselfish, concerned citizen.[100] Dillon gave up on Dublin Castle, the Connerys remained at liberty.

The end was to be quite unspectacular, a night patrol of Acting Constable Henry Burke and three policemen captured the Connerys in the house of James Fitzgerald, a weaver and reedmaker, at Kilcloher, on 27 March 1838. When Fitzgerald declined to open the door the police broke it down and found the Connerys sitting beside the fire smoking their pipes. Unarmed, they made no resistance.[101] Despite newspaper speculation that the police had been tipped off by the son of Pierce Hely's gardener at nearby Rockfield House, or that a friend of the Connerys had been seen acting suspiciously in the vicinity, ironically it appears that the Connerys had fallen victim to a routine night patrol.[102]

The Connerys were taken to Dungarvan and on Wednesday (next day), with full police and military escort, were marched to Waterford. They were afforded full celebrity status by the thousands who turned out, anxious to 'get a glimpse of the distinguished outlaws'.[103] The event could not have been designed better to reinforce the Connerys mystique: clad in their 'rich habiliments',[104] 'soon after sunset, on Wednesday evening, the two heroes entered once more the portals of the County Gaol...'.[105] Even respectable citizens were not immune and crowds of them besieged the Gaol for the next two days, hoping to see the Connerys.

The brothers were treated as convicted prisoners, and were not allowed visits from friends or their attorney while Thomas Ryan, the Governor of the Gaol, awaited government notice as to their fate. When the decision was taken to prosecute them for escaping from gaol, meetings with their attorney to prepare their defence were granted.[106] All this, together with the strict disciplinary nature of Ryan's regime rendered escape bids extremely difficult. James Fitzgerald, though he protested his innocence, was also in custody, facing a charge of harbouring and maintaining the Connerys. Despite memorials in which he cast himself as a poor weaver, whose temporary incapacity meant economic ruin, he was not granted bail.[107]

On 18 July 1838, the Connerys were brought before Judge Moore, charged with breaking out of the County Gaol. Mr. Mulcahy, the attorney who handled their defence, fell back on legal casuistry – the Connerys had not broken out rather they had simply walked out of gaol:

> Mr. Mulcahy read from Roscoe a passage in which it was laid down that to constitute a felonious breaking out of prison, it was necessary to prove an actual not a constructive breaking out; that if the gaol door was thrown open by the gaoler, the offence was not constituted; and if some of the prisoners opened the door, the others availed themselves of it, the latter was not indictable.[108]

However, Mr. Mulcahy was unable to establish precedent to the court's satisfaction. While the undergaoler James McLaughlin had been convicted of permitting an escape of prisoners, James Bruce the gaoler was adamant he did not. Moreover, although Bruce testified he had not seen who broke the inner and outer gate of the Gaol, he stated that the Connerys had been present at the crucial gate when the lock was broken. Mr. Mulcahy then threw the prisoners on the Judge's mercy. The Connerys were found guilty.

James Fitzgerald was then indicted for harbouring and maintaining the Connerys. While Constable Henry Burke deposed that Fitzgerald had stated on the fateful night 'the prisoner would not for £50 that he had a house, that the Connerys would be taken in'.[109] The defence, conducted by William H. Hassard, maintained that they had been in the house but a few minutes and had effectively taken forcible possession. Mary Feeney, Fitzgerald's servant, stated the Connerys had availed of the string on the latch to open the door, just ten or fifteen minutes prior to the police, and had bolted the door after them. The household only bolted the door when they went to bed and she said it was possible for any visitor to come in before they would be able to see them. Fitzgerald did not welcome the Connerys nor shake hands with them. When the police demanded entrance Patrick Connery had threatened to have Fitzgerald's life if he opened the door; and as anyone could term themselves police his admonition to break down the door if they were so came across as an escape from a predicament.[110]

Mary Feeney testified that the Connerys could not have been in the house without her knowledge. They had only been there once before, about six months previously, when they had come in to light their pipes. She had been afraid when they bolted the door. While she could not say whether Fitzgerald knew the Connerys, she 'knew the Connerys before anything happened to them; knew them as long as they were able to walk .... is no relation of the Connerys and never heard Fitzgerald was'.[111]

While the Protestant clergyman Reverend Richard Bermingham, to whom Fitzgerald paid his rent, gave him a good character he imposed a caveat 'Is sorry to say that, in this country, he would not be surprised to find a man of such a character harbouring felons'.[112] Fitzgerald was found guilty, but Judge Moore took into account the period he had already spent in gaol and sentenced him to another ten days. This meant an effective sentence of three months imprisonment.

On 20 July 1838, John and Patrick Connery were called to the bar for sentencing. On being asked whether they had anything to say why sentence should not be passed on them, John used the opportunity granted to address the crowded court-room. He hoped the Judge would not impose a sentence any greater than their original conviction. He noted a person convicted of the same offence at the last assizes had received a sentence of two months (presumably a reference to Thomas Kinneally). He said that his attempt to retain the most competent legal defence available had been frustrated by an attorney's duplicity:

> he gave his case to an Attorney (mentioning the gentleman's name), to have a Council, who understood better than any other matters connected with this case, and that the Attorney did not act for him although he was paid for it.[113]

The Attorney, who was present, denied it but it is unclear if John was referring to Mr. Mulcahy. The *Waterford Chronicle* did not enlighten its readers, presumably for fear of a libel action. The council referred to is surely William H. Hassard. John Connery concluded his speech from the dock with his famous castigation of Irish society and an apologia.[114] With such a forthright repudiation of the Judge's society, John cannot have hoped to endear himself with his Lordship even if it was Judge Moore.

For the liberal *Dublin Evening Post,* Moore's conduct of the Tipperary Spring Assizes of 1838 had been an exceptional breakthrough in commanding popular assent for justice. Although there had been eighty murder cases on the calendar, no death sentence had been pronounced:

> For the first time, within memory of any man living, there was no want of prosecutions. The peasantry came forward to give evidence with as little reluctance as would be manifested in the most tranquil county of England. There was no terror – no partial or organised attempt at intimidation. This is certainly a splendid triumph of the law, combined with good government, and administered with firmness and impartiality by the Earl of Mulgrave.[115]

The County Tipperary magistrates considered such liberal decisions as an invitation to anarchy, but their efforts to redress the situation drew Thomas Drummond's famous rebuke.[116] Despite the optimism of the *Dublin Evening Post,* the realities of agrarian violence in Tipperary were not so easily assuaged. What William Makepeace Thackeray termed the Tipperary fashion remained in vogue.[117]

Judge Moore, in sentencing the Connerys,

> pointed out to them the enormity of their guilt, and the desparation of the character they bore throughout the country. They were in the habit of traversing the country with arms, and to the terror of the people. He had it in his power to sentence them to transportation for life, for 14 years or 7 years, or imprisonment, but he would not give the full award of punishment, neither would he do that which appeared to be acceptable to the prisoners. He would sentence them to transportation for 14 years.[118]

As they left the dock, they turned around and made another bitter comment on the attorney's action. The writer in the *Chronicle* was convinced that it was totally undeserved. The *Waterford Mail* had taken a moral stand on the Connery trial by declining to report it, on the grounds that its readership knew enough of the brothers' notoriety.

As if the Connerys had not impinged enough on the popular consciousness, their leaving of Waterford proved momentous and an occasion for allegations of police brutality. On August 25, they were taken from the County Gaol for the last time and placed by Thomas Ryan, the gaoler, on a car. They travelled down into the city to the mail coach office on the Quay, there to board the coach for Kilmainham. It proved a tense affair. The police, anticipating trouble, had been reinforced from the County and were deployed with fixed bayonets, the mounted police had swords drawn. The castigation of their subsequent action by Maurice Lenihan, the editor of the *Waterford Chronicle:* 'the brutality and ruffianism of these over paid peace preservers', resulted in a full investigation by the City Aldermen.[119] The inquiry lasted from 9 September to 14 September 1838. It heard allegations of assaults by the police on innocent sightseers. It appears that the mounted police, in particular, had indulged in overuse of the flat of their swords. The police countered by mentioning random stone throwing and the invocation of Carrickshock.[120] They also cast aspersions on the sobriety of their supposed victims.

In Thomas Ryan's submission to the Inquiry, he detailed the tumultuous welcome the Connerys got from the crowd. When they appeared out of the gaol the crowd, of about 1,000, shouted 'huzza to the Connerys, success to the Connerys...'.[121] The Connerys responded by taking off their hats. Modestly he continued by describing how he instructed the Connerys to keep quiet. When the police grew alarmed following the smashing of a pane of glass, Ryan, as a veteran of the Clonmel Penitentiary, quietened them by saying he had seen worse in County Tipperary. On cross-examination he stated he had never before seen sympathy being expressed by the people for convicts. However, he then unleashed the 'horrible' Connery plot; 'One of the Connerys told witness there was a conspiracy to take his, witness's, life as also to take a gun from the gunroom and to shoot the gate porter...'.[122] The Connerys would then break open the gate and escape. Ryan agreed that most of the people on the day were just curious and that there was no attempt made to rescue the Connerys. He was sure, however, that if any opportunity had presented itself they would have availed of it. Ryan went no further than the coach office, where the Connerys were transferred from the car.

In the coach they sat with their backs to the horses, facing Head Constable Francis Gannon and a lady passenger, who was thought to be English, and had just arrived on the Cork coach. She caused a minor panic when she let down the coach window to allow a man to put in his hand. The Connerys, according to Gannon, did not appear to know him and Gannon got the police escort to pull the man back as he was under orders to prevent any communication with the Connerys.[123] Alexander Doyle who performed this task said that he had smelled drink on the man and had heard the name 'Holohan', but did not see any mounted policemen strike Houlahan, as alleged by Houlahan himself and John Cleary, another witness. Doyle said that he considered the attitude of the crowd to be passive but 'from the sympathy expressed for the Connerys, that the people would assist them if they attempted to escape'.[124]

The *Waterford Mail* defended the police action solidly:

> it was their duty to prevent any, even the slightest attempt at a deviation from their orders, and in preventing a mob from closing round the vehicle which contained the prisoners, and conversing with them, perhaps to receive further instructions in crime, they only did their duty, for the non-performance of which they would have rendered themselves liable to punishment. From what we saw they acted as became them.[125]

The results of the inquiry were passed to the Government. According to the *Chronicle,* the police and their friends had attempted a whitewash of the facts: 'The case set up by the police cannot fail to strike the readers with astonishment'. Thomas Ryan, the gaoler, with his Connery plot, had been brought forward 'to create a sensation' and, presumably, confuse the issue at hand.[126]

When the coach collected the mail at the post office, the Connerys left Waterford for the last time. On 8 September 1838 they sailed from Kingstown on the convict transport *Elphinstone:*

> Agus chuir na Conairigh thar na farraigí dtí na New South Wales.
>
> (And the Connerys were sent over the ocean to New South Wales).[127]

The Quay at Waterford (after Creswick) c.1840.

Chapter 5

Irish Obituary

Thus, the Connerys were parted from their own society but their society proved determined not to forget them. In folklore, music (traditional air) and song (three) a memorial was fashioned which befited the cultural heritage of Sliabh gCua. The Connerys were portrayed as the ultimate role models, their education and hospitality badges of exemplary social development. In contrast, those who betrayed them had displayed an immaturity, which demanded condemnation in this world and the next:

> *Mo mhallact ort is léir ort, a rascail bhradaigh bhréagaigh,*
> *Nára fada an lá go n-éagfair gan bhaochas Mhic Dé;*
> *Is tú ghlac an bhreab go h-éasca is a dhearbhaigh an t-éitheach,*
> *A chuir na Conairigh thar tréan-mhuir ó Bhoth a'Dúin na gcraobh.*[1]
> (A curse be upon you lying, thieving traitor.
> May the day soon come when you die without God's grace
> You took the bribe confirming your false favour
> And sent the Connerys for ever from Bohadoon *na gcraobh*).

However, a historian must treat such a commemoration with caution, for a little incident can be fashioned by an artist into a great tale. Thus not alone has it to be established whether the Connery memorial was based on fact, but also the extent to which it served as a useful literary device around which local artists embellished their craft. This work attempted to examine the substance behind the memorial and thereby satisfy the first condition.

The Connerys' story embraces the first forty years of the nineteenth century – the most extraordinary part taking place in the 1830s. The brothers were heirs both to a powerful family tradition and to the rich cultural heritage of Sliabh gCua. The former impressed on Patrick, James and John the need to preserve social position, the latter provided a particular cultural assuredness. By 1829, only a few acres in Bohadoon remained to sustain a 'glorious' Connery past and widespread economic distress reinforced the precariousness of their position. The brothers rejected a *spailpín fánach* (itinerant labourer) future and resorted to violence to preserve the remnants of the Connery patrimony. Though they ultimately failed in their objective, the Connerys' efforts afforded them hero-status in Irish oral tradition.

When they donned female clothing to attack the woodranger, Maurice Hackett, they embraced the Whiteboy tradition and attempted to prosecute it to the fullest extent. Similarly, they were not half-hearted in their membership of the Poleen faction, to the extent that John was charged with the killings of David Tobin and Patrick Brien. Thus, it was as the representatives of the two traits of the Irish peasantry most feared by the dominant society that they came before the courts.

In this alien environment, John, in particular, displayed a remarkable self possession which saw him acquitted on three occasions. John's command of English enabled the brothers to manipulate the judicial system and, most importantly, to understand proceedings.

However, nemesis, came in the form of Thomas Foley, the agent on the Holmes estate. Foley, the attorney, was an upholder of the very law the Connerys rejected. He secured their eviction, but the Connerys replied by letter, threatening his life and personal property. They intimidated the tenant who replaced them so that he fled. Foley reacted swiftly and succeeded in having James convicted for the Hackett episode at the Spring Assizes of 1835. Similarly, John and Patrick were convicted at the following assizes for forcible possession, where they displayed a contempt for the proceedings which infuriated Foley. Firstly, they attempted to strike an outrageous bargain – if both were acquitted, and James pardoned, all brothers would leave Ireland. When this was rejected, John shocked the court-room by threatening Foley.

While James was successfully removed to New South Wales, John and Patrick escaped from the Clogheen bridewell. Then, as heavily armed men, they threatened violence unless the verdict of the court was overturned – only a pardon could secure the life of Foley and his brother. The new Under-Secretary of State, Thomas Drummond, mobilised all the resources at his disposal to deal with the Connery threat, which in the worst possible outcome would envisage the brothers leading a peasant uprising.

For almost seven months John and Patrick outwitted the police, indulging in psychological warfare, personally dealing with an alleged informant, Sylvester Greaney, and culminating in a gun battle near Dungarvan. During this period, they drew enormous support from their own community who provided them with shelter and also obstructed the efforts of the police. It appeared that even the expertise of the best policeman in Munster, Chief Constable Carroll, could not prevail against the brothers' ingenuity. In demonstrating the apparent ineffectiveness of the judicial system and police, they undermined the administration of law and order and threatened its credibility. A pragmatic local gentry gave the

Connerys money to emigrate and thereby remove a dangerous subversive example.

However, they were betrayed in Waterford by the tailor Patrick McGrath, rearrested and lodged in the County Gaol. Undismayed, the brothers organised and directed a successful jail break, leading twelve of their fellow inmates to freedom and thereby securing the dismissal of the wily Governor, James Bruce. The bullets of the police could have ended the Connerys' lives near Cappoquin, but they survived to send their famous letter from Liverpool.

This piece of ingenuity achieved some respite from the police pursuit, but surveillance on the ports combined with their own notoriety to ensure the Connerys could not leave the country. They chose the accession of Queen Victoria to reopen negotiations with Dublin Castle, but were no longer prepared to use violence as a bargaining lever. As three of the most notable people in Waterford, John, Patrick and Henry Villiers Stuart met in the Park at Dromana on 21 October 1837. The Connerys were not prepared to surrender unconditionally. In an apparently hopeless situation, the Connerys spent their last months of freedom beset by worries over loss of popular support, as illustrated in the Hearn affair. They were recaptured at Kilcloher twenty two months after escaping.

On his last appearance at the County Waterford Assizes, John Connery denounced the nature of Irish society and branded an attorney a thief. Defiant to the end, the Connerys rejected the authority of the judicial system and its servant. However, even they could not prevail against the power evident in the fixed bayonets and drawn sabres of the nervous police at Waterford on 25 August 1838, as the brothers were removed to Kilmainham.

Thus, the desperate attempt to save a particular Connery ethos ended in complete failure, but the new mystique which the brothers had created far outweighed the loss of those few acres at Bohadoon. John might well have appreciated this subtle irony in New South Wales.

The ample material which the Connerys provided for artistic inspiration ensured their primacy over artistic form. Nevertheless, portrayal of the Connerys as social paragons would not be accepted unless there was consensus that they epitomised desired characteristics. Indeed, it was only by equating the Connerys with their own society that the now anonymous authors were able to capture the breadth of the Connery impact. By choosing such an effective representation they ensured that as long as that society was still desired the Connerys would be recalled.

In the *Emergence of Modern Ireland*, Cullen identifies two aspects of Irish life which distinguished it from the European norm at the beginning of the nineteenth century – its pattern of hospitality and its diet.[2] Modernisation would involve a progression towards the European parallels, the hospitality became less lavish, the central role the potato played in diet -

Prátaí is do oiche, prátaí meán lo,
Is do n' éirionn i meán óiche,
Prátaí a gheobhainn³.

(Potatoes for my evening meal, potatoes for my lunch,
And were I to arise at midnight,
Potatoes I would munch).

altered radically by the Famine. It is significant that in the three songs about the Connerys whose purpose were '*á móladh 'is á gcaoineadh*' (praising them and lamenting their fate), the themes of hospitality, food and drink are openly linked with the Connerys.⁴

Sé a dtigh a bhíodh go buachach, go fáidhiuil, fáiltiuil, fuarmach,
Geal-chuporach, mo bhuaireamh, fá mhór-chuid bhfeóil.
Lucht taistil cnoc is sléibhte agus straigiléirí aonair,
Bheadh a leaba agus a mbéile agus féile 'n-a gcóir.⁵

agus

Bhíodh an saigdear milis, láidir á riar i dteach na sárfhear;
Bhíodh an Eaglais gach féile ar staeision go hard;⁶

(Their homestead neat and tidy oozed welcome from within,
Bright cupboarded, I ween with lashings of food.
The travellers of hill and mountain and the lonely vagrant found therein,
A welcome to a bed and the fare was good).

and

(This used to be a house of good cheer with potent cider aplenty
Every feastday, the clergy came for an excellent station).

On these indices of social behaviour their performance is depicted as impeccable. Moreover, should the Connerys ever return, the effect is perceived almost in millenarian terms.

Má thagann sé chun crích 'dóibh go bhfeicfeam arís iad,
A bpardún glan ón Rí acu is iad á insint dúinn faoi shó,
Cruinneoimid ina dtimpeall gan spleáchas do na peelers,
Is beidh ár gcornán dí againn go haoibhinn á ól.

agus

Beidh againn glór na píbe, ceol, spórt is aoibhneas
Ó mhaidin go dtí an óiche is ón óiche go dtí an lá.
Beidh na bairillí ar a bhfaobhar againn is sinn ag fáscadh lámh a chéile
Agus sláinte gheal na hÉireann ní thaoscfaimid go brách,⁷

(Should the day ever dawn that we again see them,
Granted King's pardon and living in peace,
Without spies or peelers, we'll gladly surround them,

And toast to their health and their life a new lease.

and

We'll celebrate with music with sport and with pleasure,
From morning till night and again from dusk till dawn.
We'll drink and rejoice the whole time at our leisure,
And toast our dear old Ireland again and again).

Finally, in the crucial area of morality the Connery memorial will not accept any questioning of the actions of '*na sárfhir*' (the great men), the justness of which is obvious to all.[8]

> *Is go bhfuil 'fhios ag gach aoinne nach rabhadar cionntach riamh in aon chor,*
> *Ach ag seasamh 'na gceart féineach is gan é acu le fáil.*[9]
> (Everyone knows they were above reproach,
> Fighting only for their rights which were denied).

Similarly, a story collected in the 1940s begins;

> *Níor robálaithe iad sa i n-aon chor do réir mar d'airigh mise sean daoine a rá. Bhíog ag baint an talaimh díobh san eagóir, agus lámhadar leis an máistir nó leis an agent ...*[10]
> (They weren't robbers by any means as I can vouch from evidence gleaned from old people. They were being unjustly deprived of their land and they fired at the landlord or at the agent ...)

Such moral certainty about the Connerys ran contrary to the doctrines of the Catholic Church, not to mention those of the civil authorities. It is only through examining the Connery experience that the limitations of the social control exercised by both institutions become apparent. Only then is a fuller comprehension of the above assessment possible.

Contemporary journalism openly conceded to the Connerys their status, while at the same time being unequivocal on their moral and social disapproval of the brothers' stance. In the sensational 'Interesting Particulars', it is recorded how the Connerys spent an evening incognito with a Clashmore publican and the gormless local police sergeant.

> The evening was spent in great conviviality – the Sergeant in adducing other proofs of the tranquillity of his district did not forget to mention that the Connerys had gone off – whilst he told many a pathetic tale of his own adventures by flood and field while they remained in the country.[11]

While a letter writer to the *Chronicle*, who styled himself a Constant Reader, termed this incident a complete fabrication; it still captures the essence of the Connery impact. The material which does exist in the Irish National Archives establishes that, unlike the journalists of the *National Police Gazette* who embellished and some say created the heroes of the American West, there was more than substance for the Connerys' claim to such status. Moreover, the travel writers, Mr. and Mrs. S.C. Hall in 1841, succeeded in getting the name wrong and referred to them as the Connollys, surely legends were to be in the making.[12]

Ultimately, the Connerys' impact derives from the vicarious thrill they offered their own society. When the brothers go on to champion the values of their own society, that of the small farmers and labourers of the Comeragh-Monavullagh uplands, they abrogate to themselves the mantle of the Caravats and Shanavests. The Connerys, with their seal skin caps with tassels, rich habiliments, and even the sword which was taken from them in Waterford, are dressed consciously in a manner which recalls Nicholas Hanley or Paudeen Gar.[13]

They then displayed a fearlessness in their dealings with the forces of law and order which few members of their own community possessed. This daring derived from the Connery skills in improvisation, literacy, guns and English – talents not common, even in Sliabh gCua. These abilities enabled the Connerys to escape being hanged by the courts or shot dead by the police, the retribution which members of their own community expected for those who challenged these institutions. Experience demonstrated that those who emulated the Connerys would share the fate of the unfortunate Kiely and Morrissey. By helping the Connerys, members of their own society participated, relatively safely, in the brothers' attack on the status quo. Such an association, led to greater appreciation of the Connerys' sacrifice in affirming that society's values.

The Connerys did not alone confront the magistracy, the police and the courts, they also ridiculed them. Through humour and black propaganda they attempted to discredit the values of a society which was alien to them. They would have opposed their own eviction had they known when the sheriff was coming. Similarly, by inspired information, they manipulated the police pursuit until they had reduced much of that body to exhaustion. Sir Richard Keane, whose attitude to agrarian violence cost him a popular political career, was claimed by the brothers as the man who got them back their clothes. They also publicly exonerated James Bruce, the Governor of the County Gaol, of any culpability in their escape from Clogheen. On his final appearance at the Waterford Assizes, John Connery made a barefaced request for consistency in sentencing, when he noted that a person [Kinneally] had received two months at the last assizes, for escaping from the County Gaol. All these Connery examples served to affirm their own community's belief in the superiority of their own values. Thus, John Connery's famous courtroom pronouncements on Thomas Foley and Irish society were a logical conclusion of the brothers' efforts.

Moreover, the values which the Connerys were asserting and defending had come under renewed pressure in the 1830s. The Melbourne Administration in Ireland and the upper and middle class Catholics shared a determination to achieve a more effective social control. Attitudes to agrarian violence and factions as displayed in the Comeragh-Monavullagh uplands were a powerful barrier to this aim. In particular, such attitudes cut across attempts by the new Catholic political leadership to mobilise the peasantry.

In 1841, three years after the Connerys had gone, John O'Donovan captured the essence of the gap between this society and the Catholic middle classes. A disputation over the age of the church at Knockboy, in which the natives showed little deference for O'Donovan's superior antiquarian knowledge, was followed by a walk over the mountains of Sliabh gCua and a visit to the Barony of Glenahirey. He concluded:

This is the most Irish county I have yet traversed and I am sorry to say, the less interesting in its antiquarian remains and the people are not as enlightened as any county in Connaught.[14]

The failure to conform to the perceptions of the dominant society was most marked in the institution of the faction fight. For Cornewall Lewis this represented a state of social flux:

Now the Irish factions mark a state of feeling which has not yet made the first step which has not risen from sympathy with ones clan, to sympathy with ones order.[15]

Chief Baron Joy at the County Waterford Spring Assizes of 1834 had little time for sociological evaluation of the Poleens and Gows. 'These factions are engaged in brutal hostility against each other, without any real cause whatsoever'.[16] Moreover, he undertook to do all in his power to suppress these practices 'which assumed such nonsensical names'.[17] The political commentator Alexis de Tocqueville, as seen, met no one who offered a differing interpretation of the factions, neither was he witness to any dramatic faction revelation in court.

Rather, members of the factions tended to perform as in the Carrick-on-Suir group with much hilarity and incomprehension. 'It was great fun yer honour but damned if we know what's it all about'.[18] Any inkling of organised rural class conflict, as Roberts has demonstrated in a major reappraisal of the role of the Caravats and Shanavests, would have caused alarm among their worships and provoked judicial severity. There may be parallels in which the American Slaves developed the happy-go-lucky, simple Sambo character to mask their true feelings from their masters or, as is the case in numerous Mafia trials, where defendants have never heard of such an organisation.

In reporting a conversation which took place between the economist Nassau Senior and the Secretary of the Poor Law Commission, de Tocqueville says that when Revans was asked about the state of morality in Ireland he commented; 'There is no other Country where it is more difficult to get the truth out of a man'.[19] A great deal more work remains to be done on the Poleens and Gows to discover the truth: did they mirror the same socio-economic distinctions as the Caravats and Shanavests or were they merely no more than what contemporary observers depicted them as. It may be possible that the social consciousness of the Connerys was shaped and honed by their Poleen associations, previous to their embracing the Whiteboy tradition.[20] If this was so, it would open up major areas of historical reassessment:

> Factions fulfilled a rather different function in peasant life from that of the Whiteboy societies, allowing a ritual and perhaps cathartic release of tensions. They had no other objectives than the opposition to another faction. It is in their networks and lessons in bringing together of large numbers of people that they may have contributed to Whiteboy organisation. The Whiteboys in contrast were engaged in more serious business which required that organisational solidarity be achieved by the taking of secret oaths, the maintenance of 'cells' and a close identification with the aspirations and interests of the social class which spawned them.[21]

Whatever the case, by 1838 Thomas Drummond and Dublin Castle had at its disposal a fully centralised police force, capable of exercising a greater degree of control in areas like the Comeragh-Monavullagh uplands. The new Irish Constabulary were more than able to make up for the scarcity of resident gentlemen and enforced a new order, particularly at fairs. These developments could count on the support of a Catholic political leadership, which was conscious of the need to remove any barriers to its own pre-eminence in the rural community. Thus, the Connerys can be perceived as opposing the forces of modernisation, on behalf of their own community.

In the final analysis, the Connerys are in the best heroic tradition even though our picture of them is necessarily incomplete; for as Broeker points out:

> Over the years, a seemingly endless number of documents relating to Irish disorder were deposited in the official repositories of London and Dublin. Much of the material still exists; collectively it constitutes the history of a war compiled from the records of only one of the combatants.[22]

The Connery memorial provides a wonderful balance, but the limitations of the oral medium precludes the same amount of detail as can be found in the official repositories. Despite this, it still captures the breadth of the Connery impact.

They belong to that particular Gaelic tradition which personalises great social upheaval. Just as Alastair Mac Colla Mac Donnell epitomized the English Civil War in Ireland and Scotland,[23] the Connerys represented the 1830s in Waterford. Similarly, as it was impossible for the Gaelic World in the mid-seventeenth century to identify with Montrose,[24] it was impossible for the Connerys' society to identify with the new Catholic political leadership or the reforming Whig Administration in Ireland. Thus, neither Daniel O'Connell nor Henry Villiers Stuart could replace the Connerys.

The world of the Connerys' did not long survive their passing. It was to be decimated by famine, emigration and, ultimately, linguistic change. The Connery songs were not translated into English, presumably because the social context of small farmer and labourer was not appropriate to the dominance of the strong farmer, which followed the Famine. One, at most two, generations in the Comeragh-Monavullagh uplands continued to be Irish-speaking after the Famine, and it is their survivors who provided the Connery folklore for the Folklore Commission collectors in the 1930s and 1940s.

Finally in one of the Connerys songs the audience is exhorted:

Le linn an Aifrinn bígí ag agallamh 'gus ag guidhe chum Dé
Ar na Conairigh a thabhairt abhaile chugainn ó na New South
Wales.[25]

(Think of us at Masses and in your prayers
That God will send the Connerys home again from New South Wales).

In treating the Connerys whether as *na sárfhir* or as the greatest 'wretch'(es) that 'ever disgraced existence', it is hoped that a worthwhile dimension has been added to Irish historiography of the 1830s. However, to bring them home means a journey to New South Wales.

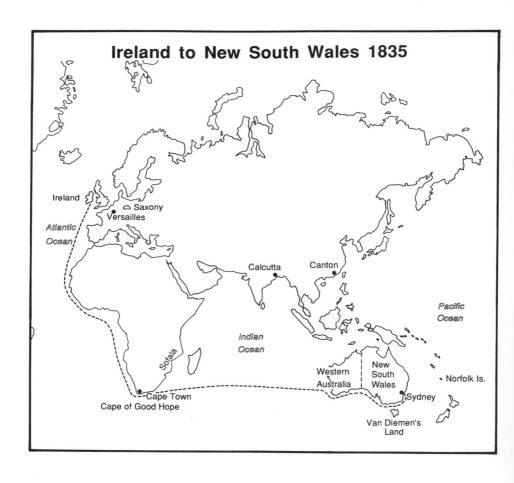

Ireland to New South Wales 1835

Ireland

Saxony

Versailles

Atlantic
Ocean

Calcutta

Canton

Pacific
Ocean

Indian
Ocean

Sofala

Western
Australia

New
South
Wales

Norfolk Is.

Cape Town

Sydney

Cape of Good Hope

Van Diemen's
Land

Chapter 6

James – The Leaving of Ireland

James Connery was marched to Cove. The journey took three days and fresh military escorts were provided at Clonmel and Fermoy. The convicts were taken down to the quay and transferred by boat to the hulk *Surprise*, which lay at anchor in the harbour of Cork.

James and the others waited while the women in the Convict Depot at Cork made up their clothes for the voyage:

> *Tá jacéid gairid á dheanamh ó mhaidin dúinn a's triús dó réir,*
> *Culaithe farraigí ní nár thaithigheamar i dtúis ár saoil,*[1]
> (We are being fitted with short jackets and trousers to match,
> Seafaring clothing our style do not match)

The summer heat exacerbated the cramped conditions within the hulk. There was little shade to be had in a stationary vessel. A company of soldiers had to come from the shore to quell a feud between the Munster and Connacht prisoners which was carried on with 'swords' made of pointed iron hoops. Despite the segregation and disarming of the convicts, the *Surprise* was perceived to be 'internally boiling with the most wicked and malignant passions of its depraved inmates'.[2]

The convict transport *Hive* arrived at Cove on 9 August 1835.[3] She had already collected some prisoners at Kingstown and carried £40,000 in bullion for the Commisariat at Sydney. The 485 ton vessel was fifteen years old; built entirely of English oak and had made a successful convict run the year before.[4] Now the owners had entrusted the contract to a new captain, Thomas Nutting. The Government had installed Surgeon Anthony Donoghue of the Royal Navy and a convict guard, composed of twenty nine rank and file of the 28th Regiment, to ensure that the cargo arrived intact.[5]

James Connery was given his new clothes and new shoes. This finery consisted of a sleeved vest and trousers lined with baffety, a pair of socks, a shirt and a jacket lined with shirting linen, with a lined baize cap.[6] He also received a towel, some needles and thread to maintain his outfit and a bag for his possessions. James had few belongings, for the Connerys had lost everything – there was no money to entrust with Surgeon Donoghue for safekeeping.[7] When James was led below deck on the *Hive* and took his leave of Ireland, poverty on top of imprisonment beckoned in New South Wales.

The Cove embarkation was completed on 23 August, bringing the total on board to 250, of which two were military prisoners. It officially ended when Major Edward Trevor, Medical Inspector and Superintendent of Convicts, sealed the Lord Lieutenant's warrant with a convict list in a tin case, in the presence of the Captain who was to deliver it to the Governor of New South Wales.[8] The *Hive* sailed on the morning, catching a fair northwesterly breeze.[9]

Captain Nutting steered a direct course, making no landfalls, and successfully rounded the Cape of Good Hope. Surgeon Superintendent Anthony Donoghue encountered no great problems with disease, as he applied experience gained on two previous voyages. Indeed, it appears the convicts enjoyed better health than the soldiers, for they accounted for only five of the eleven cases noted in his medical journal.[10] However the *Hive* was sixty two days out of Cove when Michael Desmond died of pneumonia contracted during his apprenticeship to a glass manufactory. He was only eighteen and had been convicted of burglary at the Cork City Spring Assizes.[11] His burial at sea reminded James Connery and the others that perhaps not all were destined to reach New South Wales.

Although the *Hive* made a speedy passage, the Captain was having problems with navigation. At noon on 6 December 1835, he informed an officer they were in 129 degrees east but they reached Cape Otway, 143 degrees 11 east, the following morning.[12] However, Nutting brought them through Bass Strait successfully and sailed up the east coast of New South Wales, passing Montague Island at noon on 10 December.[13] He then fixed a course which he believed would take the *Hive* '12 or 14 miles outside Cape St. George'.[14] The first mate, Edward Canney, felt this was too close to land with night coming on, but the Captain ignored these reservations and retired to his cabin. The night was dark and cloudy with a fresh breeze which acted as a strong in-draught. At ten o'clock the third mate noticed something white on the starboard bow and fearing breakers, he rushed to get Canney. Canney ran on deck and ordered the helmsman to put the *Hive* to port, but it was too late she struck, under full sail and 109 days out of Cove.[15]

Death by drowning appeared to face all on board: 'The confusion and terror that prevailed, at this time is not to be described'.[16] The Captain 'had lost all presence of mind' as it appears he had lost two ships already.[17] Moreover, the *Hive's* crew was short and he had two illegal passengers on board.[18] Surgeon Donoghue and Lieutenant Lugard deposed Nutting and placed Canney in charge to the screams of the women and children of the convict guard. Panic drove the prisoners close to mutiny, but Patrick

Maloney, who had served on an American whaler, was able to calm his fellows and disaster was averted.[19]

The *Hive* was not to share the fate of the *Neva* which, on her 125th day out of Cork, in the early morning of 13 May, struck a reef near King Island in Bass Strait. 225 perished and only six of the 151 women who embarked at the Convict Depot survived, of the fifty five children on board, none was saved.[20] Although the *Hive* was aground in 'heavy breakers', she was within her own length of the shore.[21] She had ended up in a deep bight to the southwest of Cape St. George, between it and Sussex Haven.[22] *The Australian* observed: It is providential that she went on shore at that particular spot – if, at almost any other neighbouring point, she would probably have gone to pieces with the loss of every life.[23]

At daylight the Captain resumed authority and had the jolly-boat launched, but she was swamped in the heavy surf. Worse followed when the boatswain, John Edwards, was dashed against the *Hive's* stern and drowned while attempting to save one of his men who was in difficulties. Finally Edward Canney, who had taken a prominent part in the rescue operations, persuaded Nutting to launch the long boat.[24] The women and children and part of the guard were the first to be landed. Eventually, the prisoners were brought ashore and James Connery found himself on a sandy beach in New South Wales.

Ensign Kelly, with the assistance of friendly Aboriginals, reached the property of Alexander Berry at Coolangatta that evening.[25] Sir Richard Bourke, Governor of New South Wales, received the news in his residence at Parramatta, the next day, and dispatched *H.M.S. Zebra* with the Revenue Cutter *Prince George* immediately, to secure the convicts and bullion. The Sydney to Newcastle steamer, *Tamar*, was engaged also and sent, with a detachment of the 17th Regiment, to reinforce the convict guard.[26] Alexander Berry's schooner, *Edward*, completed the rescue flotilla. As it was, James Connery and the other Irish felons 'encamped among the sandhills' made no effort to escape.[27]

Jervis Bay provided the safest anchorage and was within an isthmus of land from where the *Hive* was stranded for 'no prudent Commander would risk his vessel in the Bight'.[28] The convicts were used to transfer most of the bullion and government stores overland. The irony of handling a fortune in silver and gold so soon upon his arrival would not have escaped James Connery. The *Tamar* arrived back in Sydney on 16 December 1835 carrying Anthony Donoghue and 106 prisoners.[29] It is likely that James Connery was among a further ninety four on board *H.M.S. Zebra* which reached Sydney on 18 December.[30] If Patrick and John had heard of this in Ireland they would surely have made much of the fact that it took an English warship to bring their brother to New South Wales.

Attempts to refloat the *Hive* failed and the rest of the convicts were brought to Sydney early in the new year.[31] However, James Harding who had been ill with dysentery during the voyage, died on the beach. He had been tried in Limerick for larceny and transported for seven years.[32] All the bullion, mail and government stores had been salvaged when Captain Nutting returned for the rest of the cargo on 15 January 1836. The schooner *Blackbird* anchored in the Bight, but a sudden gale drove her on the shore and she was wrecked quite close to the *Hive*.[33] Sir Richard Bourke ordered an inquiry into the loss of the *Hive* and the board, which sat in Sydney on 11 February, censured Nutting's conduct after leaving Montague Island.[34] Official disapproval ensured that the certificate for the completion of the convict contract was not issued until 20 March.[35] The cost of hiring the *Tamar* and *Edward*, £435 10s 0d, was later deducted from the *Hive's* owners freight claim and it is assumed Nutting was never again entrusted with a command.[36] Well could the bight be called Wreck Bay.

Chapter 7

Government Man

By 1836 the colony of New South Wales was well established. The British invasion, which began with the penal settlement at Sydney in 1788, had overwhelmed the native society and culture of that part of the Australian continent.[1] Disease, alcohol and the transformation of the landscape had destroyed the Aboriginal world, unlike Ireland where invasion and colonisation had still left a land half-won.[2] The penal nature of the new society was quickly eroded by the gaolers, in particular the New South Wales Corps, who diversified into farming and trade. They were willing to defend their stake in the new land against convict and Governor alike. In 1804 the Corps crushed an Irish rebellion at Castle Hill and, four years later, deposed Governor William Bligh, in the Rum Rebellion, when he attempted to curb their illegal privileges. Similarly, the gaoled added to the complexity by having children, the currency lads and lasses, and ultimately becoming free themselves (emancipists). Such was the rapid evolution of their antipodean experiment that the British Government ordered a review of its future direction. In 1819 Commissioner Bigge had envisaged a society dominated by large graziers.[3] This was much appreciated by the group around the now disbanded Corps, which fancied itself as a new aristocracy. The rest of the free population was not disposed, however, to become mere sheepherders and cattle minders. An agenda was set for the next thirty years.

New South Wales began as a planned society whose culture was English and whose religion was Anglican. This was upheld by the almost dictatorial power of the early governors. However, the presence of a large Irish Catholic minority, which was mostly of convict origin, complicated matters. The latter were a majority in their own land and were not disposed to acting like a minority in the new. Not alone were these Irish on the lower rungs of the social ladder but some of them were agrarian agitators and men of 1798.

Thus, any concessions to be won for Irish Catholics involved political action against the status quo and, because of their composition, would necessarily entail social action. Hence, in the confined closed-in world of the early colony, Irish Catholics were recognised as a political threat and there was a widespread fear that the men of '98 and all the horrors of the French Revolution were perpetually imminent. Samuel Marsden, the Anglican Chaplain, put his finger on this by saying that if any concessions were given to Catholics the colony would cease to belong to the Crown in one year.[4] The Castle Hill rising of 1804 seemed to illustrate the point.[5] The result of all this was that Irish Catholics were put outside the pale of New South Wales Society and thereby became a great dynamic for change.[6]

Individuals did, however, achieve high office as in the case of James Meehan, Surveyor General and Irish Catholics did acquire property as emancipists or free settlers. Indeed, Waldersee argues that quite a lot of property was owned by Catholics in 1828. He maintains that in earlier days, intolerance, in theory, was 'balanced out by considerable accommodation in practice'.[7] Nevertheless, as in the case of the Penal Laws in eighteenth-century Ireland, people were not grateful for their uneven and intermittent application when they believed the principle was unjust. Similarly, the wrangling over the colony's Catholic priests left a bitterness which was not easily assuaged. While the liberal, Anglo-Irish Governor, Sir Richard Bourke, from County Limerick, pursued a policy of unprecedented conciliation in the 1830s, which anticipated and mirrored that of the Melbourne Administration in Ireland, it ironically coincided with developments within the colony which revived all the fears about Irish Catholics.[8]

Irish Catholic alienation added an important component to the great social divide between the would be bunyip aristocracy[9] and the rest of New South Wales. The pure merinoes dominated the Legislative Council, a body nominated by the Governor, set up in 1825, and used their capital to gobble up crown lands by purchase or squatting, whichever proved most expedient. William Charles Wentworth, an antipodean O'Connell, led the opposition which demanded a much wider share of the political and economic opportunities in the colony. This conflict did not become violent, not least because New South Wales – unlike Ireland – was a frontier society and the discontented could seek their fortunes beyond the settled districts.

James Connery, as both a convict and an Irish Catholic agrarian rebel, began at the bottom of New South Wales society. His prospects were poor for he had arrived too late. Although the transportation system was at its height in the 1830s the percentage of the population which was convict was declining rapidly. After 1821, as Hughes pointed out, very few ex-convicts made big fortunes.[10] The best that James could look forward to, if he survived the penal system, was to fade into 'hard working respectable obscurity'.[11]

When James stepped ashore at Sydney Cove he became the

responsibility of John Ryan Brenan, the Irish Acting Principal Superintendent of Convicts. He was lodged in the Hyde Park Barracks, to await assignment. Since James could neither read nor write English and was only a 'farm servant', there was no question of him being classed as a 'special'.[12] 'Specials' were held in the hulk *Phoenix,* in Sydney Harbour, while they awaited removal to Port Macquarie. In keeping with the times the authorities believed that the educated convicts – in particular those involved in white collar crime – posed a greater threat than others and needed to be segregated from them, under direct government control. All other prisoners, after public works requirements were met, were assigned to private service. Thus, New South Wales was a vast open prison, in which the convicts worked out their sentences and, thereby, made an immense contribution to the colony's economic development.[13]

By the 1830s, most of the convicts were being assigned to private service. The era of ambitious public developments, presided over by Governor Sir Lachlan Macquarie, 1810-21, was long past and the saving of government money had become a priority. In a sample of 200 prisoners from the *Hive,* only three were designated 'specials', five were reserved for the government and 182, including James Connery, were assigned to private service.[14] A Board for the Assignment of Servants supervised the allocation of convicts, using a quota system relating to an applicant's acreage and livestock. James was assigned to William Edward Riley of Raby. He was handed over to Richard Jones, Riley's agent in Sydney, and, after a journey of twenty nine miles along the Great Southern Road, he arrived at Raby on 13 January 1836, just in time to help with the harvest.[15]

Raby was a holding of 3,200 acres and was one of the finest properties in New South Wales. It was an appropriate monument to the contribution which the Riley family had made to economic development and agricultural innovation in the colony. The family had already succeeded as migrants in England. In the early part of the eighteenth century William O'Reilly left County Cavan and established himself at York. His family preferred the more anglicised 'Riley' one of whom, George, became a prosperous London bookseller and freeman of the city.[16] Two of George's daughters married officers in the New South Wales Corps and this induced their brother Alexander, to move to the colony in 1804. Alexander Riley quickly combined government office, land grants and trade to make a fortune. Although associated with those involved in the Rum Rebellion, wisely he took no part and became one of the main building contractors for Sydney Hospital when Governor Macquarie restored direct rule. Alexander also helped to found the Bank of New South Wales in 1816, an imperative for someone whose trading networks linked Sydney with Calcutta and Canton. However, in 1817 he left for London with his family and never returned to New South Wales.[17]

Despite his best efforts, Alexander was unable to achieve effective management at such a remove. His younger brother, Edward, who had run the Calcutta link moved to New South Wales and became a major pastoralist in his own right. Tragically, however, he shot himself in 1825[18] . Yet Alexander persevered and had great success with his programme of importing the finest European livestock into the colony. His most spectacular achievement was with sheep selected and purchased from the Elector of Saxony's flocks which arrived in New South Wales in 1825 and 1828.[19] These became the famous Raby Rams, whose bloodlines influenced the development of the Australian merino, and whose 'importance to the Australian pastoral industry is probably greater than that of any other flock'.[20] Alexander was awarded a land grant of 5,000 acres with another 5,000 to follow when the project was complete, for his services to New South Wales. He also brought in Skeleton, the great Irish thoroughbred stallion who, because of a bad trainer, never reproduced the form of the Curragh of Kildare, 1823-6, in England.[21] Alexander also introduced Neapolitan Pigs and in 1832, together with his only son William Edward, arranged for Angora-Cashmere crossbred goats to be brought from Versailles, France.[22] William Edward Riley accompanied the goats home and, with the death of Alexander in 1833, the young 'Anglo-Australian' became proprietor of Raby.[23]

James Connery had left the traditional farming methods of the Comeragh uplands for the most modern agricultural expertise in New South Wales. Here, there was no entrenched, impoverished tenantry to obstruct scientific advance. As an assigned convict James had to be fed and clothed by his master. He was also bound to follow his master's instructions, but he was only in his custody and any misdemeanours had to be brought before the local bench. James still remained the responsibility of the Superintendent of Convicts Office and while he was spared incarceration in a prison, the traditional penal system was preserved in the places of secondary punishment. James was never to experience the particular horrors of Cockatoo or Norfolk Island.

At Raby, James became one of the twenty or so 'government men' who made up most of the workforce. They were supervised by an overseer who was responsible for issuing the weekly rations. In the first week of February 1836 James received ten pounds of second class flour, eight pounds of beef, two ounces of tea, one pound of sugar, one and a half ounces of tobacco and four ounces of soap. However, on 25 February he drew his last rations at Raby and set out with twelve others for Cavan on the Murrumbidgee to help William Edward Riley realise his dream. Cavan lay almost 150 miles to the southwest, just outside the settled districts.[24]

Cavan station comprised almost 70,000 acres on the southern bank of the Murrumbidgee. It originated in the Saxon sheep land grant which was taken up at Narrangullen in 1831. William Edward Riley purchased a further 1,920 acres to the east, on Mountain Creek, from Henry Manton in 1834. However, he was not concerned about the lack of title to the crown lands which lay between the Goodradigby River, to the west, and Mullion Creek, to the east, so barely one sixth of Cavan was truly freehold.[25] William Edward built a beautiful house and filled it with 'elegant cottage furniture'.[26] Similarly, no expense was spared on the outbuildings or farm machinery. He even installed a cannon to communicate with his friends in Yass, ten miles away. When he did travel to Yass, it was invariably in an English phaeton (carriage), with two postillions. Thus, at Cavan William Edward spared no efforts in reviving the glorious past of the O'Reillys' of East Breffney.

Cavan for James meant harder work. Although he had been a woodranger at Bohadoon, this did not make the clearing of gumtrees any easier. The size of the station meant that the cattle and sheep were easily lost. The colonial magistracy, mindful of their own livestock, invariably imposed sentences of fifty lashes on those found guilty of such lapses. Despite its size, the workforce at Cavan averaged only thirty men, who had to look after a small property near Lake George, which was about fifteen miles to the east, also.[27]

However, James acquired the dubious advantage of trial by Irish Catholic magistrates, for in the area around Yass some of that community had considerable wealth and formed part of 'The strong Catholic bias of the southeastern areas of New South Wales'.[28] The most prominent were Henry and Cornelius O'Brien from Hollymount, County Mayo, whose progress in the colony had been underwritten by their uncle, William Browne, who had made a fortune in trade in Calcutta.[29] While at Cavan James ensured he never met the O'Briens on the Yass bench.

Although William Edward Riley cultivated an aristocratic image, he shared his father's reservations about the merits of a bunyip aristocracy. He had joined the Australian Patriotic Association, which sought a directly elected legislature as a result of which the dominance of the pure merinoes in the Legislative Council would be ended. There is no doubt that as a magistrate and prominent member of the Southern Association for the Suppression of Stock Stealing, he would have had definite prospects in such a legislature. His status was further enhanced by the very successful Yass Plains Races on 20 and 21 October 1836, which he organised. It was the first race meeting in the district and even James Connery was affected by the excitement and preparation for the event, though he did not share in the claret and champagne. On the last day of the races William Edward Riley laid the foundation stone for Yass courthouse and spoke of his optimism for the future.[30] He died tragically, six weeks later, at the age of twenty eight.

The manner of his death at Cavan on 4 December is unclear and it is not inconceivable that James Connery was aware of some of the details. Yass folklore offers conflicting accounts. One version has William Edward shooting himself after a drinking bout, with the suspicion of malign influence by one of his acquaintances. The other has him taking too much laudanum as a sleeping draught, after a friend had lost an arm in an accident with the cannon.[31] However, a document, purporting to be his will, turned up later in which everything was left to his daughter, Christiana Riley, but this was challenged successfully by her mother.[32] The Rileys had three children: Alexander Raby, Christiana and Margaret, who was born after her father's death. William Edward's remains were brought to St. Peter's Anglican Church in Campbelltown, close to Raby, and he was buried in the adjoining cemetery on 31 December 1836.[33]

Cavan had lost its architect and James Connery and the other were consigned to the monotony of station life. 1836 had been very warm and dry along the Murrumbidgee and 1837 brought little change. Cavan began to be run down as Stuart Alexander Donaldson sold cattle and sheep to clear his dead friend's debts. This friendship had developed from that of their fathers which had been cemented by trading interests and was underlined by Stuart Senior acting as executor to the estate of Alexander Riley. Young Stuart had come from the silver mines of Mexico to manage his family's trading interests in Sydney. He disposed of the Riley bloodstock, even selling Skeleton not to mention the English phaeton, in raising £9,000 to satisfy all of William Edward's immediate creditors.[34] Nevertheless, he was determined to maintain the property which also included Ousedale and Malton, in Appin, not far from Raby, so James Connery remained at Cavan while his future and that of the system which brought him there was considered in London.

The concern of the Melbourne Administration with penal reform, already manifest in the abolition of the Irish hulks, led to the setting up of a select parliamentary committee on transportation in 1837.[35] The report of the Molesworth Committee, when presented to the Commons in 1838, indicted the whole system, but especially assignment to private service, which it perceived as corrupting both master and man. It recommended the ending of transportation to New South Wales and the settled parts of Van Diemen's Land urging, instead, that prisoners be kept at home and housed in modern penitentiaries and for those who had to be sent abroad similar institutions could be built in places like the Falkland Islands. Hughes argues that the Committee was more of an inquest than an inquiry, and the speed with which first assignment and then transportation were ended in New South Wales seems to support this.[36]

In condemning the system, the Molesworth Report highlighted the moral shortcomings of the colony in a manner as insensitive as

Commissioner Bigge had done. Many in New South Wales were outraged and blamed the Catholic Church, not least because of Reverend William Ullathorne's damning evidence, which concentrated on atheism and sodomy but also because it was felt that Daniel O'Connell had influenced his Whig allies. With a Bishop of New Holland, albeit an English Benedictine, in place since 1835 and now an 'apparent link between Botany Bay Popery and Botany Bay Whiggery'[37] – Irish Catholics were perceived to be menacing the colony, once more.

The year 1838 brought no relief to Cavan and the district around Yass, which broiled under 'a cloudless blue sky for many weary months'.[38] The drought imposed great hardship on James Connery and his fellow 'government men', as fodder and water for the remaining cattle and sheep grew scarce and Lake George began to shrink. Stuart A. Donaldson decided that the Riley Estate could no longer afford to farm directly and he leased Cavan to Major Edmund Lockyer, for a term of five years, in July.[39] It is assumed that their agreement was such as to ensure James Connery and the others did not have to be surrendered to the Principal Superintendent of Convicts Office. Thus, James Connery was still at Cavan in September, when Bishop John Bede Polding visited the station as part of a pastoral sweep around Yass. He had come to Yass, officially designated a town the year before, to consecrate a Catholic cemetery and lay the foundation stone for St. Augustine's Church.[40] Bishop Polding aspired towards an Australian Catholic Church which would be fully integrated into that society and whose needs would be served by Benedictine monasticism. While the O'Briens of Yass were sympathetic to such a vision the less wealthy Irish Catholics, including those at the bottom of the scale such as James Connery, were not. These were encouraged by their own clergy, whom O'Farrell had termed 'the most influential Irish immigrant group', who believed that the combative model of home was most appropriate to the new land.[41] This position was reinforced by an influx of Irish Bounty Emigrants, 1838-41, which provoked a severe anti-Catholic reaction and thereby denied Polding any initiative for his policy.[42] Although he persevered, further Irish immigration and Irish clerical manpower ensured he had little hope of success.

Meanwhile, there was a severe curtailment of the system of assignment during the later part of 1838. On 15 August, Governor Sir George Gipps announced that assignment of male convicts to towns was to be ended from 1 January 1839 and tightened up the quota system. A further measure, on 18 December 1838, ensured that all newly-arrived male convicts had to be kept in government service for at least six months and, thereafter, could only be assigned at their superintendent's recommendation. While this had little immediate effect on James Connery at Cavan, the same could not be said for his brothers Patrick and John.

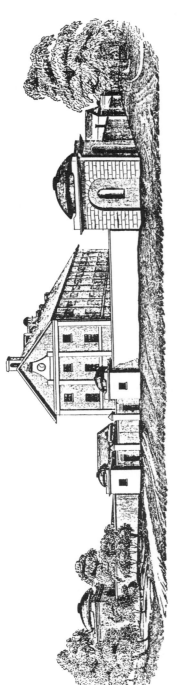

HYDE PARK BARRACKS.

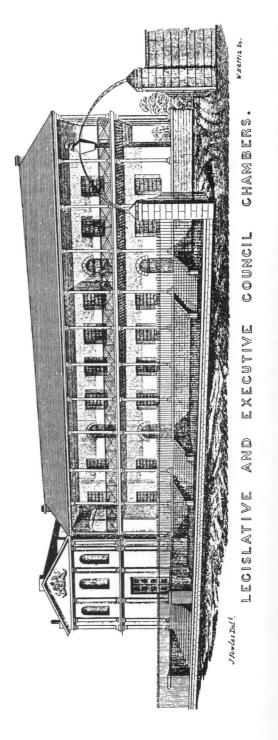

J.Fowles Del.

W.HATT & Sc.

LEGISLATIVE AND EXECUTIVE COUNCIL CHAMBERS.

Chapter 8

Lachlan Swamp, Cavan and Port Macquarie

It is perhaps indicative of their reputation that John and Patrick Connery spent only two nights in Kilmainham Gaol, from whence on 27 August 1838 they were removed to the convict transport *Elphinstone,* in Kingstown Harbour.[1] Like James three years before, John and Patrick and 230 fellow prisoners received their ocean finery. Then, Major James Palmer, Inspector General of Prisons, sealed the Lord Lieutenant's warrant and the prisoner list in a tin case in the presence of Captain Thomas Fremlin.[2] The *Elphinstone* sailed on 8 September.

This was her third convict run, as she had already completed two successful voyages to Van Diemen's Land under Captain Fremlin. She was smaller than the *Hive,* at 425 tons, and although built in Bristol in 1825 had been recently extensively repaired.[3] The Surgeon Superintendent, Dr. Alick Osborne, was making his eighth voyage, having experienced both Irish and English transports.[4] The Connerys and the others had an excellent chance of landing safely in New South Wales.

For the first two weeks Patrick Connery lay ill with 'debility'. He had no sooner recovered when John was placed under Dr. Osborne's care, with headaches and, later, a sprained foot. Although he suffered a more severe bout of fever in October, its twelve day treatment presented no problems for the Surgeon Superintendent. Indeed, Dr. Osborne's medical expertise and the captain's concern for the prisoners' welfare ensured that there was no serious illness throughout the voyage. The Connerys spent Christmas Day at sea and, three days later, the *Elphinstone* completed her passage of the three oceans when she arrived safely in Sydney Harbour.

The healthy arrival of the Connerys and the rest in New South Wales struck an observer as 'an unprecedented occurrence', on the morning he watched them come ashore.[5] It is presumed Patrick and John immediately sought word of James even though communication may have taken place already, given John's grasp of the postal system. However, while James may have received an Irish letter at Cavan it is difficult to see where he could have got the money for a reply. Now there was to be no reunion, for Patrick and John were kept in Sydney. They were put in charge of the city's water reserve, the Lachlan Swamp, positions of some responsibility, which allowed a great deal of personal freedom.[6] These jobs were crucial in ensuring the Connerys did not come into conflict with the penal system in New South Wales.

The Lachlan Swamp, which was a great natural reservoir, lay two miles to the east of Sydney. It acted as a sump for the run-off from the surrounding hills and retained rainwater in a spongy, sandy soil which served as 'a splendid natural filter'.[7] Pure water, which occured at depths of four to five feet, was drained into an underground aqueduct, Busby's Bore, and on to Hyde Park. This tunnel was the brainchild of John Busby, Colonial Surveyor, and had taken its convict workers ten years, 1827-37, to complete. The system provided the city with an excellent water supply which did not fail in the long drought of 1838. The Connerys adapted quickly to their marshy wilderness and cleared paperbarks and she-oaks to build a house and fence a vegetable garden. They also developed good relations with their master, Lieutenant-Colonel George Barney, R.E., the Colonial Engineer. Most significantly, it appears that Patrick and John were able to exploit the wild cattle of the swamp as a source of income. This aspect of their existence in New South Wales is preserved in the Irish folklore:

> *thógadar lota talún le hais Sydney, lota talún fiáin, coillteach. Dheineadar é a romhar agus a réabadh, a shaothrú agus a dhaingniú nó go raibh sé chomh inchurtha le haon talamh dá fheabhas. Bhí ráille adhmaid timpeall leis acu agus bhí comhlaí ann anseo agus ansiúd. D'fhágaidís na comhlaí sin oscailte d'oíche ionas go dtagadh na beithigh allta isteach ó na sléibhte chun a saint a agairt ar na barraí. Nuair a bhídís istigh, dhúnadh na dheartháireacha na comhlaí ón taobh lasmuigh agus bhídís ag gabháil timpeall lasmuigh den ráille ag déanamh caradais agus caidrimh leis na beithigh allta agus á bpeataireacht go dtí go mbídís mínithe agus oilte acu. Ansin dhíolaidís iad agus d'fhaighidís mórluach orthu.[8]*

(They took a tract of land alongside Sydney, a tract of rough wooded land. This they dug, prepared, tilled and cultivated until it was as arable as any good land. They enclosed the tract with a timber railing, leaving gated openings here and there. The gates were opened at nightime, as an invitation to wild cattle coming in from the mountains to sample the taste of crops. When a number of animals had gone through the brothers closed the gates from the outside and from there proceeded to make advances of friendship to the animals. They cajoled, petted and patted the wild cattle until they became docile and tame. They then sold them for a goodly sum.)

Neither were the brothers found wanting in their work. They ensured that the Swamp's watercourses were kept clean and clear and maintained the waterworks in good running order. It was to take the development of local government in Sydney to replace them.

Meanwhile, the colony had begun to slip into economic depression which was to have serious consequences for the new tenant of Cavan and, indirectly, for James Connery. The drought of 1838-9 was followed by falls in the prices of wool, beef and mutton. Bushrangers menaced the district of Yass but the 'wild colonial boy' future was not for James Connery.[9] This coincided with a great revival of the Wiradjuri people along the lower Murrumbidgee, about 200 miles to the west. Led by their tall Brian Boru, they had successes initially, but the poisoning of water holes and massacres left them completely defeated by 1841.[10] The unprecedented conviction and execution of seven Whites in 1838 for the murder of twenty eight Aboriginals at Myall Creek had changed little.

Major Edmund Lockyer, a Devonman, was a better soldier and explorer than a farmer. In the early 1840s, when he began to experience financial difficulties, his main concern was to preserve Lockyersleigh, his fine estate near Goulburn. In 1841 he withdrew most of his flocks from Cavan.[11] The effect on its 'government men' is unclear, but it seems likely that only a few of the workforce were retained. In April 1841 Stuart A. Donaldson wrote to the Colonial Secretary seeking the replacement of three convict servants who had been removed from the Riley Estate.[12] If James Connery was among them it would help to explain the granting of his ticket of leave at Port Macquarie in 1844.

The depression shook the confidence of the pastoral interests already reeling after Molesworth. The divisions between the pure merinoes and the emancipists were quickly forgotten, as ruin faced all. Indeed, Henry O'Brien saved many when, in June 1843, he perfected and advocated the boiling of sheep for tallow.[13] The liberal aspirations of the Australian Patriotic Association did not survive the new alignment as the restrictive franchise was now in vogue.[14]

Sydney received its last convict transport, the *Eden,* on 18 November 1840. Assignment to private service reduced to a trickle in 1839 and ceased on 1 July 1841.[15] The Bounty Emigrants filled the gaps in the labour supply left by the convict workers, but generated much hostility because many were Irish. Those who feared being swamped in a flood of Irish Catholic poor overlooked or failed to distinguish the substantial Protestant minority among the arrivals. One young bounty emigrant from Cappoquin was to brighten the existence of John Connery.

Ellen English was seventeen when the *China* left Waterford on 28 July 1839.[16] She travelled with five members of her family and the voyage was pleasant, despite the loss of two infants and a woman. They stopped at Cape Town for seven days to take on fresh provisions, vegetables and water. There was school on board for the children and the adults relaxed in the evenings with music and dancing. Sydney was reached on 20 December and the passengers – 210 Catholics and 50 Protestants – disembarked. Ellen and her sister Catherine secured a year's employment as housemaids with Mrs. Gurner, in O'Connell St.[17] Ellen met John Connery and although she may have known him in Ireland she could not but be aware of his heroic status. Ellen became pregnant and their son Patrick, was baptised in St. Mary's Cathedral on 16 May 1841.[18]

John could have married Ellen but only with the consent of the Principal Superintendent of Convicts. This permission was not sought and the circumstances of their eventual marriage help little to enlighten us in this regard.[19] The Catholic Church in New South Wales was very conscious of its missionary situation, thus St. Mary's baptismal register does not distinguish the marital status of an infant's parents. Little Patrick Connery died in November, at Frazier's Lane. His coffin was brought to St. Mary's where Fr. Patrick A. Hogan, who had baptised him, read the funeral rites.[20] Even in an age inured to high infant mortality, John's and Ellen's loss would have been difficult to bear.

Meanwhile there was major developments just outside the Lachlan Swamp. On 8 February 1841, Lieutenant-Colonel George Barney began construction of the Victoria Barracks, which would remove the military from the fleshpots of Sydney. The work took seven years and, in the process, the Connerys acquired many new neighbours, including French-Canadian victims of the imperial system. These *Patriotes* were among those who declared Canada independent in 1838, but their rebellion was crushed and fifty eight were transported to New South Wales for an indefinite period.[21] It is believed some were responsible for the fine stoneworks at the barracks, even though all were pardoned by Queen Victoria in 1843. Although the workforce was mainly convict, there was also an influx of free quarrymen, masons and carpenters out of which grew the village of Paddington.[22]

The Connerys received many visitors at the Swamp, but were particularly careful of 'government men' on the run. These bolters or bushrangers sought to avail themselves of the Swamp's excellent cover. Some lost the Connerys' confidence, spectacularly so in September 1842, when the brothers apprehended four convicts after a fight in which John was stabbed. They brought them to the Hyde Park Barracks, not feeling bound by any code to those they could not trust. This proved timely, for the brothers' tenancy of the swamp was soon threatened by the advent of democracy to Sydney.

New South Wales shed its penal character with the election of the Sydney City Council on 1 November 1842. The franchise was much wider than the elections of 1843, which returned twenty four of a new thirty six member Legislative Council, created under the Constitution Act of 1842.

Thus, the pastoral interests had little influence on the city body, which included butchers, publicans, builders and tanners, whereas they dominated the new Legislative Council.[23] Sydney was given control of its water supply and two men were appointed to the Lachlan Swamp whom the town clerk envisaged would take over the Connerys' house and garden once the brothers were removed. However, Lieutenant-Colonel Barney wanted them to remain, to protect the government's land and quarries and they were given authority to prevent the removal of soil and stone. On St. Patrick's Day 1843, the Connerys wrote to Barney, seeking approval of this role until such time as they came up for tickets of leave.

Sir

Having heard that two freemen have been appointed by the Corporation to supercede us in the charge of the Lachlan Swamp, from which the City is supplied with water, and as we have been in charge of the same since our arrival in the Colony and during that time (now 4½ years) have given satisfaction to the Head of the Department & the public, we would most humbly Entreat that we might be permitted to remain in charge of the grounds & quarries belonging to the Government until we may be entitled under the regulations to receive Tickets of Leave.

In making this application we would humbly take the liberty of reminding you that we apprehended in September last 4 runaways and lodged them safely in Hyde Park Barracks where they were dealt with and in the act of apprending them that one of us (John) received a stab from a knife. that Carts are now continually removing loom and lately we stopped three men from quarrying stone in the Government Quarries.

Should we be permitted to remain. We would humbly beg leave to assure your honor that every exertion on our part should be taken not only to assist in preserving the water but also in preventing any one in any way trespassing on the Government property or removing soil or stone therefrom.

We have the honor to be Sir
Your most humble & obedient Servants,
John Connery
Patrick Connery.[24]

Governor Sir George Gipps granted Barney's request and the Connerys were also to retain their house and garden.[25] Moreover, the tenancy was considered so important that the terms of their tickets of leave were later changed to allow them to continue.

James Connery was the first of the brothers to receive a ticket of leave. It was granted for the district of Port Macquarie on 20 March 1844, nine years after his conviction at Waterford.[26] The ticket of leave was an integral part of the penal system, conferring a qualified parole on its holder, as a means toward his gradual rehabilitation into society. It meant that James was now free to work for himself and acquire property, but he had to remain within the district. Similarly, he had to present himself at periodic musters, where the local magistrates monitored his progress. He was also required to attend weekly worship 'if performed within a reasonable distance'.[27] James was left in no doubt that the ticket was a guarantor of his behaviour. Any trouble and it would be revoked making him an ordinary prisoner, once more. However, he coped with the permanent insecurity and was never deprived of his partial freedom.

The expertise which allowed James Connery to set up as a road contractor was probably acquired on the road from New England to Port Macquarie. This link was intended to transform the penal station into a natural entrepôt for the wool-producing Tablelands. James may have been among the convict drafts of April/May 1841 who were brought in to help with its construction.[28] The work involved the upgrading of eighty five miles of bridle path and was difficult and dangerous. In 1843 an observer, describing its progress, wrote:

> The road winds through a fearfully broken country, hitherto considered impracticable. For about 10 miles it is cut through thick bush, and for twenty more it has been scraped out along the sides of ravines and precipices.[29]

Convicts sent to Port Macquarie as incurables and later deemed convalescent were added to the road party for W.N. Grey, the police magistrate, considered it 'more conducive to their health than to have them crowded in the Barracks'.[30] However, shortages of manpower and the economic depression ensured that the road was not a success. Those wool drays which did come down from New England found a port with a troublesome bar. Port Macquarie became a casualty of the ending of transportation.

A quiet backwater, with limited opportunities for employment, was not the ideal environment for a ticket of leave holder, but James Connery managed somehow to earn a living for four years. On 14 August 1848 he was granted permission to take up employment in New England.[31] He would work for his old master at Cavan.

John and Patrick Connery was granted tickets of leave on 8 August 1844, six years after their conviction, the minimum requirement under the regulations.[32] They received an excellent recommendation from Captain Joseph Long Innes, the police magistrate attached to the Hyde Park Bench, as having 'evinced a disposition on all occasions to assist the police in the execution of their duty'.[33] The brothers appeared to have broken completely with their Irish past.

Chapter 9

Tickets of Leave

John and Patrick were now required to move to Bathurst, the district of their tickets. However, the Connerys did not wish to leave the Lachlan Swamp. Their tickets were successfully altered, on 14 April 1845, but in anticipating a favourable outcome it appears that the brothers never set foot in Bathurst.[1] This was all made possible by their good relations with the authorities.

Meanwhile, John and Ellen had another child, James, who was christened in St. Mary's on 11 December 1844. Unlike little Patrick, he survived infancy. However, his parents did not marry. If the child was not reminder enough of his absent uncle, John had made the acquaintance of Stuart A. Donaldson. The administrator of William Edward Riley's estate had just returned from England, having left the colony in 1841. His absence was disastrous for Cavan, not to mention his own affairs. In 1842, Major Lockyer, the tenant, allowed the squatting licence for Cavan Run to lapse. In 1843, the Commissioner for Crown Lands issued the licence to Edgar Beckham, a fellow Commissioner. Donaldson was unable to overturn this on the grounds of propriety, so, for the want of £10, the dream station of William Edward Riley was reduced to about 13,000 acres. Indeed, it appeared that even that would be lost, for the government were now pressing for the payment of quit rent on the 10,000 acre Saxon sheep land grant. The Riley Estate was in no position to pay, but a resourceful Donaldson appealed the matter to Lord Stanley, the Secretary of State for the Colonies and, ultimately, ensured it was not resolved for seven years.[2] Although Donaldson's own merchantile and pastoral interests had been hit by the economic depression, the bad management which followed his departure to England did not prove terminal. John Connery met a man who had substantial interests in Port Philip, Bathurst and New England with ready access to the colonial establishment.[3]

The Connerys were now free to acquire land but by the mid 1840s most of New South Wales had been occupied. Security of tenure was as great an issue as in Ireland, but in New South Wales it was the demand of the rich and powerful. These were outraged by the legislation of 1842, which set a floor of £1 an acre for the sale of crown lands. They used the financial powers of the new Legislative Council and also lobbied Westminster, who had control over the land, in an effort to gain a permanent hold over their squattages. Victory came, in the form of leases granted under the measures of 1846 and 1847.[4] Moreover, when land had to be purchased the pastoral interests bought the water source (peacocking) and thereby restricted the market for the remainder to themselves. Their success was complete when, in the next decade, the control of crown lands was vested in the local legislature. In such a system there was little room for small farmers from Bohadoon. John eventually bought some land, but he was fated not to enjoy it for long.

The Connerys' partial freedom coincided with disaster in Ireland. In 1845, the blight struck the potato and began *An Gorta*, that cycle of starvation, disease, evictions and emigration, which lasted well into 1849. If ever there was a need for *na sárfhir* at home it was now, but, at the remove of New South Wales, the brothers were powerless to intervene. Agrarian violence proved unable to halt the catastrophe, rather traditional resistance was broken by death, the removal of public works and the British Army. The Connerys' world ceased to exist, its passing marked by a failed revolution.

On 16 September 1849 Joseph Brenan, the radical Young Irelander, led a rising at Cappoquin. It was to have coincided with an outbreak in County Tipperary, but James Fintan Lalor and John O'Leary called this off because of their tiny forces. Lalor, in his belief that the land of Ireland belonged to all of the people of Ireland and his strong defence of tenants rights, came closest to peasant common law. The rebels, armed with pikes and a scattering of firearms, attacked the police barracks, but were driven off with one person killed on each side. Brenan and most who took part escaped, but fourteen were arrested and transported. Of these, one died in Spike Island Prison, two had their sentences commuted to two years imprisonment, four were sent to Bermuda and seven to Van Dieman's Land.[5] The latter never received the recognition or the superior prison treatment associated with the fiasco of Ballingarry, the year before.[6] Were the Connerys now ever to return it would be as traumatic as Oisín's return from Tír na n-Óg.

Meanwhile it appears that John Connery had undergone a religious conversion, for on 23 September 1848 he was married to Ellen by Reverend James Fullerton, at the Scots' Church, Pitt Street. John signed the register to the effect that he was a member of or held Communion with the Presbyterian Church of Scotland. Ellen did not sign, but her sister Honora Orr and husband James witnessed the marriage.[7] Although the celebrant was later accused of running a marriage shop and narrowly escaped conviction on a criminal prosecution James Connery and his

84

sister, Mary, were raised as Presbyterians.

It is unclear how John Connery first met James Fullerton, but it may have arisen from his prominence in the temperance movement. Fullerton, born in Aghadowey, County Derry, was ministering in Benburb, County Tyrone, when he became one of four Irishmen to answer John Dunmore Lang's call to the Australian mission. He arrived in 1837 and, after a short period in Windsor, moved to Sydney and to a congregation drawn mainly from the North of Ireland. By 1842, he had his own church at Pitt Street and played a prominent role in the deposition of Lang by the Synod of Australia. This produced a split and Fullerton proved adept at the in-fighting that followed. The fray was further complicated in 1846 by the setting up of the Free Church-inspired Synod of Eastern Australia which left three bodies contending for the allegiances of the Presbyterian faithful.[8] Fullerton had enhanced his reputation within this community by his 'Motives to the Due observance of the Sabbath' and his critique of Puseyism, the Anglo-Catholic movement in the Church of England. In the former, he did not neglect the Irish example:

The happiness of a country may at any time be fairly estimated by the extent to which the Sabbath is sanctified by the inhabitants. The influence which the profanation of the Sabbath has on the character and feeling of a people is clearly manifest in Ireland. In Ulster, in which Presbyterianism prevails, the Sabbath is generally kept as in Scotland, but in the south of the island it is openly profaned ... In Ulster where the Sabbath is generally kept holy, peace, industry and good will prevail; but a large portion of the people in the south are proverbial for indolence, rapine and violence. Nor ought we to suppose it could be otherwise.[9]

Despite this Fullerton set no limits for his mission:

The great object at which he aims is to bring perishing sinners to the Lord Jesus Christ; and those who have been in the habit of attending his Ministry are aware that his desire is to inculcate the truth without alluding to sect or party....[10]

Irish Catholic agrarian rebels such as John Connery were not beyond redemption.

While it is unlikely that Patrick welcomed his brother's conversion, he continued to reside with John and Ellen at the Lachlan Swamp. The remaining restrictions on their freedom in New South Wales were lifted on 20 December 1848, when both were granted conditional pardons by Governor Sir Charles FitzRoy. They were now free to go anywhere in the world, but the pardon would be revoked if they returned to the United Kingdom of Great Britain and Ireland. This exclusion would lapse on 16 August 1852, when their sentences expired.[11]

John and Patrick could now at last, as in their offer to Thomas

Drummond, move to the United States or the British Colonies, but they chose to continue at the Water Reserve. Ten years in New South Wales were not easily abandoned, not to mention brother James.

On 14 August 1848, James Connery was issued with a ticket of leave passport which allowed him to remain in the New England service of Dr. John Rowland Traill for twelve months.[12] However, Traill was but a manager for Stuart A. Donaldson, whose holdings comprised the adjoining stations of Clifton (70,000 acres) and Tenterfield (100,000 acres). Both were named after places associated with Donaldson's family in Scotland.[13] While Dr. Traill was James's immediate boss, he also had to contend with Robert Ramsay Mackay, Donaldson's associate and erstwhile partner.

Like Cavan, Tenterfield ran both cattle and sheep, but Clifton was given over completely to sheep. James found himself among 670 cattle and 20,000 sheep at Tenterfield, with a further 12,000 at at Clifton. By 1849 Donaldson was stocking almost 1,000 cattle and over 50,000 sheep, having achieved security of tenure at Tenterfield, with a fourteen year pastoral lease from the Crown. Moreover, as the elected member for Durham since February 1848, he was in an excellent position to safeguard all his interests in New South Wales.[14]

James Connery adjusted quickly to minding sheep along Weeton's Creek, at £30 a year. The sheep were dispersed in flocks of about 1,000 and were folded in yards each night.[15] James had to protect his charges from dingoes, rustlers and Aboriginals, whose belief that the Earth's bounty belonged to all was unaltered by the coming of the white man. He also had to be careful, for if found in breach of his hiring arrangement he risked loss of his ticket of leave. Moreover, his free colleagues faced fines and imprisonment under the Masters and Servants Act, designed to keep labour in employment. Their confidence was not inspired by the Court of Petty Sessions at Tenterfield where Donaldson, Traill and Mackay all sat on the bench. It appears James Connery encountered little problems while in New England for although Dr. Traill was strict and frequently prosecuted employees at Tenterfield court he was also fair.[16] His family had been friendly with Donaldson's in Scotland and, having qualified in medicine at Edinburgh, he came to New South Wales. He continued to practice but also became an excellent station manager.

On 3 September 1850 James was granted a conditional pardon by Governor FitzRoy, fifteen years after his conviction at Waterford. He was now free to rejoin his brothers.[17]

Chapter 10

Freedom and Gold

Despite outward conformity, events in late 1849 and 1850 raised doubts as to John's and Patrick's reformation in New South Wales. It all began when Governor FitzRoy visited the Lachlan Swamp. John seized the opportunity to grant himself an audience and request his excellency's help in preserving the Connery house and garden which were being threatened by Sydney Council's plans to fence the Water Reserve. The Governor told him to put it in writing, whereupon John and Patrick delivered a memorial in which they sought 'some renumeration for their services, or in lieu thereof to make them a grant of 4 or 5 acres of the crown land outside the Water Reserve'.[1] In effect, the brothers wanted payment from the day they set foot in New South Wales – a complete subversion of the transportation system.

His excellency was a bit taken aback and had the Connerys informed that there was no money available nor did he have the power to give land grants. John and Patrick knew this well for, quite apart from being an indulgence in black humour, the memorial was designed to serve as an opening gambit. On 6 February 1850 they wrote to Edward Deas Thomson, the Colonial Secretary, seeking three or four months grace at the Swamp, as they envisaged purchasing some land for a new homestead between it and the South Head Road. The letter dispensed with the usual supplicatory approach on the grounds:

> we believe our characters are so well known to the Authorities as honest hard working and industrious men since we have been in the Colony as to prevent the necessity of obtaining certificates of character.[2]

The Connerys were advised to apply to the Mayor for permission; the brothers, however, were determined to stay in government accommodation. On 28 February they wrote again to the Colonial Secretary, seeking to be allowed to occupy a vacant house at No. 1 Quarry, on the South Head Road. It was on the south side of the road, in Paddington, and had been built about 1841 by the firm who had leased the quarry from the government presumably to supply stone for the Victoria Barracks. This time

John and Patrick were successful and, following a meeting with Edmund T. Blacket, the Colonial Architect, and a visit to W.W. Billyard, the Civil Crown Solicitor, in which they agreed to vacate the premises on the former's notice, the brothers took up residence. An attempt by someone to burn the place about a week before the Connery letter helped matters considerably.[3]

The new house was but a short distance from the old home, so the brothers were able to continue their farming enterprises. However, John felt he needed an alternative source of income. He decided on a career in the police and on 7 June he applied for the position of Chief Constable at Tenterfield. He did not, of course, mention his connections in the area namely brother James and Stuart A. Donaldson, nor his extensive experience of the Irish Constabulary. John cited the apprehension of seven bushrangers while at the Swamp and his own integrity. 'My character for honesty, sobriety and industry is well known for years past not only to the public but yourself'.[4]

John had no hope of following in the footsteps of Michael Dwyer, the great symbol of Irish-Australian conformity, who had been made a constable at Parramatta in 1813.[5] It was not merely a matter of convict versus state prisoner, but of a different New South Wales. In 1850 the penal colony was finally buried, its passing marked by the firm rejection of the 'exiles', convicts who had served part of their sentences in the United Kingdom and whom the British Government hoped to pawn off on New South Wales. Moreover, the Australian Colonies Government Act, in extending the franchise and increasing the powers of the Legislative Council, provided an effective framework for the achievement of responsible self-government. Thus, it was particularly inappropriate that John Connery, a former convict, be given a position in the police.

However John's personal interest in public employment continued and, on 24 September, he applied for the crucial position of ranger on the Crown Lands in the neighbourhood of Sydney.

To The Hon. Col. Secretary

Sir

I beg leave most respectively to apply to you for the situation of "Ranger" of the Crown lands in the vicinity of Sydney as I am informed that a person is required for that purpose – I have for the past twelve years resided at the Lachlan Swamp and have had charge of that place and the land in the vicinity by virtue of orders from Sir George Gipps and Colonel Barney – I am at present residing by permission of the Government. at No. 1 Quarry and am protecting the intrusion of parties as also preventing them from carrying away wood, loom, or stone, etc.

While I have been residing at the Swamp I apprehended seven bushrangers who were tried at Hyde Park before Captain Innes. The late Sir George Gipps when in the Colony gave me permission to reside at the Swamp as long as I wished so to do and as I am well acquainted with every portion of the land I wish to obtain the Situation. My object is not so much for the salary as for a comfortable home and if appointed I am sure you will have no fault to find with me for neglect of duty or honesty of purpose.

> I am
> Sir,
> Your obedt. humble Servant,
> John Connery.[6]

The job was necessary, if only to frustrate Simeon Henry Pearce, who, since his appointment in 1849 as the first Commissioner for Crown Lands in the district of Sydney, had attempted to curb the Connerys' activities on government property. Pearce's public zeal was not uninfluenced by his attempts to recreate his home village of Randwick in Gloucestershire, England, on 'the heights above Coogee Bay'.[7] He envisaged a genteel, residential district, presided over by the occupant of Blenheim House (presumably called after the Duke of Marlborough's palace). Not alone did the Connerys contest this leadership role, but their very presence in the area was not in keeping with an antipodean English village. Relations were further strained when John acquired a little over three acres of land close to Blenheim House.[8]

John was well aware that the filling of the two positions lay with Commissioner Pearce so he mustered some impressive character references, in an attempt to sway the Colonial Secretary towards intervention. He was able to get Lieutenant-Colonel George Barney, now Chief Commissioner for Crown Lands and George Hill, Mayor of Sydney, to endorse his application. Moreover, Thomas Ryan, the Irish Chief Clerk in the Principal Superintendents of Convicts Office and Joseph Long Innes, the police magistrate wrote of his sobriety and honesty. Finally Stuart A. Donaldson M.L.A. added 'He had been known to me for the last six years. By reputation before that time. I have no hesitation in strongly recommending him to the consideration of the Government'.[9] Unfortunately, John was too late, for this submission was received on 5 October 1850 one day after Pearce had rejected John's application on the grounds that 'I see no reason (although with all deference to His Excellency) to alter my former recommendations'.[10]

Although Pearce was triumphant, he was unable to secure the house at the No. 1 Quarry to accommodate his rangers. John and Patrick ignored the rangers and continued to allow their cattle the freedom of the Crown

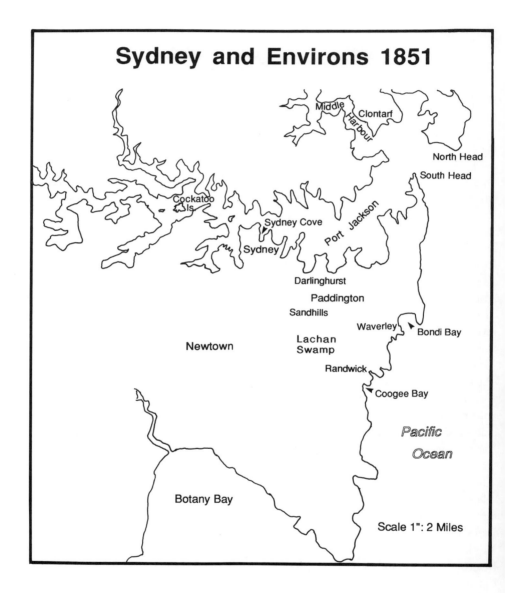

Sydney and Environs 1851

Middle Harbour

Clontarf

North Head

South Head

Cockatoo Is

Sydney Cove

Port Jackson

Sydney

Darlinghurst

Paddington

Sandhills

Waverley

Bondi Bay

Newtown

Lachan Swamp

Randwick

Coogee Bay

Pacific Ocean

Botany Bay

Scale 1": 2 Miles

Lands. The Connery cattle were particularly partial to the shrubs which bound the frail ecology of the area known as the Sandhills. Overgrazing and the cutting of shrubs made for the periodic sandstorms which inundated Sydney.[11] It was difficult to expect the brothers to intervene, since they had been superseded in their conservation function. Pearce, who claimed to have served an apprenticeship to the nursery trade, was determined to solve the problem which led inevitably to more conflict with the Connerys. However, before this took place, almost all of New South Wales went mad.

The brothers' failure in the Australian Gold Rush of 1851 ended any hope of reviving a glorious Connery past under southern skies. On 12 February 1851, Edward Hammond Hargreaves and John Lister found some gold near the junction of Lewes Ponds Creek and Summer Hill Creek. Hargreaves had been attracted to the area by the similarity of its geology to the Californian goldfields. His experience there had shown him that the quickest fortunes were not made at the end of a shovel so, when he was certain of the government reward, he gave the discovery full publicity. By calling the district Ophir, after the biblical source of King Solomon's fabulous wealth, he whetted the appetite of the entire world.[12]

Once he spoke at Mr. Arthur's Inn in Bathurst, on 8 May, the rush began.[13] The Masters and Servants Act became the first casualty of gold fever, as many of the workers left to seek their fortune on the steep and rugged banks of the Creeks, fifty miles beyond Bathurst.[14] Those who had resisted the early excitement were sorely tested by the exhibition of a forty six ounce nugget at Bathurst and Sydney, in late May, en route to the Crystal Palace and the Great Exhibition in London. In the last days of autumn John and Patrick, together with some friends, left for the diggings. Their expectations must have been high for along with the brothers' expertise in water, they carried Californian cradles which were needed to screen the material from the river beds. Moreover, *na sárfhir* would have had little worries about the rough, wild and tough nature of Ophir. However, they never reached the goldfields not to mention completing the 121 miles to Bathurst.

Disaster struck on 28 May, the day the *Sydney Morning Herald*, in a cautious editorial on gold and speculation, conceded; 'The destinies of the land are changed'.[15] The Connerys and their party, having crossed the Nepean River, made camp at Emu Plains. They were about thirty five miles from Sydney, with the Blue Mountains still to be crossed. There are few details about what followed. It appears that while they were resting a crowd from the locality approached the camp and 'insisted upon examining' the box-like cradles.[16] The visitors promptly broke one of them which led to a dispute ending in a fight. This went badly for the brothers and their friends. The Connerys were unable to combat both time and weight of numbers. All their expertise and ingenuity were unable to save John from a severe beating which seriously impaired their ability to resist the arrests that followed. Indeed, the manner of their being taken into custody is unknown. However they were 'committed for trial by the Penrith Bench for assault'.[17] The Connerys were granted bail which left them with little funds and with John in a poor state they decided to return to Sydney. Had they pressed on it is unlikely they would have returned for the trial which would have led to inevitable conflict with the New South Wales police. John's health ensured such a dangerous option could not be considered and thus there was no Australian reprise of the events which made *na sárfhir.*

John did not improve, despite the attention of Dr. Cuthill. It mattered little to him that Ophir was soon rivalled by Sofala on the Turon River. This discovery took its name from the area in Portuguese East Africa where some believed King Solomon's mines lay. Indeed on 1 July 1851, the day the Port Philip district was detached from New South Wales to create Victoria, gold was found in the Plenty Ranges near Melbourne.[18] John died on 3 July and was buried in the Catholic section of Sydney Cemetery. A funeral notice was inserted in the *Sydney Morning Herald* and Fr. John Kavanagh, who performed the ceremony, recorded John's profession as a farmer.[19] What he had been deprived of in Ireland he had at least recovered in New South Wales.

There was an inquest which returned a verdict of death by natural causes.[20] Patrick, Ellen and the children left the house on the South Head Road. The luck of the Connerys, which had lasted all of twenty years, ended when John's coffin was lowered in the sandy clay.

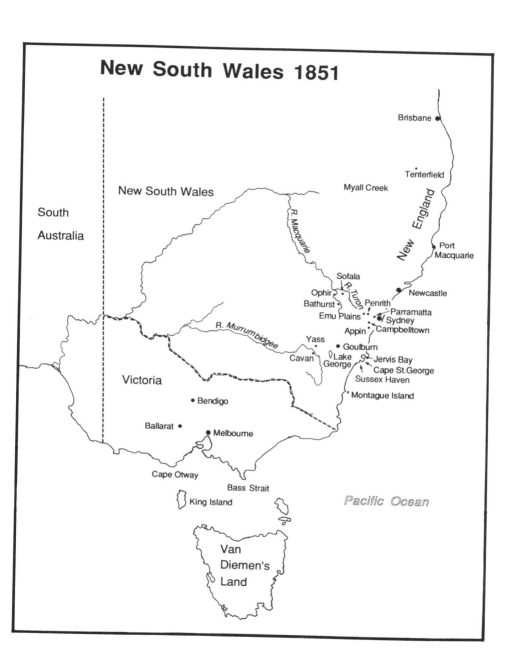

New South Wales 1851

Brisbane

Tenterfield

Myall Creek

New South Wales

New England

South

Australia

R. Macquarie

Port Macquarie

Sofala

R. Turon

Newcastle

Ophir

Penrith

Bathurst

Parramatta

Emu Plains

Sydney

Appin

Campbelltown

R. Murrumbidgee

Yass

Goulburn

Cavan

Lake George

Jervis Bay

Cape St.George

Sussex Haven

Victoria

Montague Island

Bendigo

Ballarat

Melbourne

Cape Otway

Bass Strait

Pacific Ocean

King Island

Van Diemen's Land

THE AUSTRALIAN GOLD DISTRICT.—BATHURST TO OPHIR.

GOLD-SEEKERS ARRIVING AT BATHURST, ON THEIR WAY TO OPHIR.

Chapter 11

The Last of the Connerys

The loss of John, the ablest of them all, finally ended any possibilities of a major Connery impact in New South Wales. Indeed, Patrick and James now began to think of a return to Bohadoon. This would not be financed by gold, for the new riches of Bendigo and Ballarat left the surviving brothers unmoved. Instead, they sought to acquire wealth as contractors. There was also the Connery cattle.

The conflict with Simeon Henry Pearce remained. Although Patrick had left the house on the South Head Road, he generously gave it to a friend, without reference to the Colonial Architect. An outraged Commissioner was taken by surprise, but eventually had Thomas Kinneally, with a wife and five children, put out and the house demolished. This object was achieved by reporting allegations of dancing on the sabbath and running a brothel against the new occupants, as well as drawing attention to Kinneally's wife in Ireland.[1] Pearce had less success on the Sandhills. Despite having special protective legislation passed in 1851 and securing the fencing of the area in 1853, Patrick and when later joined by James proved to be durable opponents. Indeed. on 16 October 1854, Patrick dispatched a masterful letter to Governor FitzRoy. It detailed the destruction of various government buildings, including the house on the South Head Road, and the carrying off of the stone. In the final paragraph he observed:

> As the officers of the Victoria Barracks were prevented from using any of the above, in the erection of a building for their Cricket ground by Mr. S.H. Pearce I presume the destruction of the building aforementioned to be unauthorized.[2]

Thus, in the subtle black humour of the Connerys', Patrick commented on the administration of the Crown Lands within Sydney.

Pearce had to report on these points. The Governor accepted his detailed submission as a satisfactory explanation and Patrick's complaints were deemed to be 'not only groundless but vexatious'.[3] Pearce had remarked:

> In concluding this report I beg to state for his Excellency's

information that the object of Mr. Connery is to annoy me for having performed my duty, in removing his friends from the huts therein mentioned, and for having on several occasions, prosecuted him and his brother, for destroying the shrubs and depasturing their cattle on the Sand Hills. They set me and the law at defiance and they have given me more trouble and annoyance than the whole of the inhabitants in the vicinity of the Sand Hills.[4]

Despite official approval of his actions, the Commissioner still had problems on the Sandhills. On the night of 27 December, barely two months later, the breaks or hedges erected there were maliciously set on fire. The Government offered £20 or a conditional pardon for the 'apprehension and conviction of the guilty parties',[5] but to no avail. Moreover in March 1857, 'certain evil disposed persons' removed part of the fencing.[6] Thus, it would appear that the Connerys' cattle were never short of an occasional browse on the forbidden ground.

As contractors, Patrick and James quickly benefited from the prosperity which gold had brought to New South Wales. Increased public and private expenditure and a wave of immigration led to a construction boom around Sydney. Their inability to read or write caused few difficulties for the occupants of the house opposite the Barrack Gate in Paddington. Indeed, James drew on his time at Port Macquarie when he specialised in roads. By the end of 1855 the brothers were in a position to return to Ireland. However, James was still excluded from his native land.

Although Patrick's sentence had expired in 1852, James was only a holder of a conditional pardon. On 31 December 1855, having spent twenty years in New South Wales, he lodged a petition for an absolute pardon. Unfortunately, neither his petition nor the government's consideration of it survive. The petition was refused on 12 March 1856.[7]

James must often have wondered what would have happened had he delayed his application for six months. On 6 June 1856 his old employer and John's friend, not to mention the member for Sydney Hamlets, which included Paddington, became the first Premier of New South Wales under responsible government. Stuart A. Donaldson's strong pastoral and mercantile interests had brought him great wealth during the gold rushes. As a politician who described himself as a liberal conservative he was able 'to secure a strong Catholic backing'.[8] His Ministry lasted only until 25 August. After a short period in opposition he distinguished himself in a reorganisation of government administration. By then Donaldson could have done little for James Connery, whose health had begun to fail.

James had consumption. He was sick for nine months and, despite the care of Doctors Muller and Heffernan, there was no remission. He died on 8 September 1857.[9] The wake and the funeral, even the death notice in the *Sydney Morning Herald*, served as a reminder that James was no mere inhabitant of Paddington, but a Connery from Bohadoon. Indeed, the hospitality and entertainment may well have approached that for which the songs in Ireland still praised *na sárfhir*. On 10 September, James joined John in the Catholic Section of Sydney Cemetery. Now only Patrick was left.

The last of the brothers had no wish to return to Ireland alone. Although sixty years of age there was no waiting for the grave and he continued to work as a contractor. Difficulties soon arose on a contract with the Colonial Architect to remove human and animal waste from the Victoria Barracks and other government buildings in Sydney. While not very salubrious, the job was doubly lucrative for the market gardens on the edge of Sydney were forever in need of 'night soil'. A bill for £230 was disputed by Alexander Dawson on the grounds that most of the work claimed for had not been carried out satisfactorily. Patrick pressed for full settlement, particularly as the contract had not been renewed for 1858. He got £30, on account, but when the balance was not forthcoming he instituted legal proceedings against Dawson. The paradox of an ageing agrarian rebel and former convict sueing a high government official would have delighted the old world of the Comeragh Uplands.

Wisely, Patrick sought the recovery of the small sum of £20. The case was set for the Court of Requests in Sydney on 19 April 1858, but it is unclear whether the case was ever heard. Patrick called on Dawson on 12 May and accepted £70 as a final payment.[10] The Colonial Architect had the cheque made out since 20 February but it seems unlikely Patrick took a loss. Rather he compromised on the compensation for loss of contract.

The scale of Patrick's financial interests may be inferred from a transaction preserved in the Land Registry. On 9 November 1857, Robert Bourke, a butcher, made over lands at Shadforth St. to Patrick, subject to redemption by the payment of £350 and interest within one year. Bourke proved unable to meet these terms, so the property became Patrick's. He had it sold by public auction in December 1859, where it was purchased by James Hanrahan, another butcher, for £150.[11]

Despite all this, Patrick was not joined by his nephew, rather young James became a butcher. Although John Connery had died a Catholic his wife and children remained Presbyterian. Ellen Connery kept up the ties with Dr. Fullerton and the Pitt Street Church and ensured the Connery uncles had no influence on her children's religious upbringing. In 1865, Ellen's pastor, as Moderator of the Synod of Australia, helped to reunite the Presbyterian Church in New South Wales. The following year, the Connery Presbyterian link was confirmed when James was married, by Dr. Fullerton, to Elizabeth Urquhart of Waverley. She was eighteen, the daughter of a quarryman, and had left Roxburgh in Scotland as a six year old.[12] Similarly, Mary Connery was also married by Dr. Fullerton, in 1875, though she later joined the Church of England of her husband, Richard Dummett.[13] He was a currier, living in Waverley, who had emigrated from the West Country. As New South Welsh Protestants, the younger Connerys were safe from that panic of anti-Irish Catholic hysteria which gripped Sydney in 1868. The same could not be said for their uncle or for their mother, with her Irish accent.

On 12 March 1868 Irish revolutionary violence, the spectre of Castle Hill, revisited New South Wales, when Henry James O'Farrell shot Alfred, Duke of Edinburgh, at Clontarf on Sydney's Middle Harbour and exclaimed, 'I am a Fenian, God Save Ireland'.[14] Queen Victoria's youngest son survived but the attack was a severe setback to those in New South Wales who craved imperial recognition and respectability. This, together with a genuine fear of Fenianism, inspired by their actions in Canada, Ireland and England, and reinforced by the recent arrival of sixty two prisoners in Western Australia, produced an atmosphere ideal for an aspiring politician to exploit. Henry Parkes, Colonial Secretary and Minister for Police, rushed a draconian Treason-Felony Act through the legislative assembly on 18 March, in which it now became an offence to refuse a toast to the Queen. He stuck with the Fenian Scare, even though doubts soon arose about O'Farrell's mental state, not to mention his Fenian associations.

In the tense period following the shooting and the opening of the Dubliner's trial, extending until his execution at Darlinghurst Gaol on 21 April, many Irish in Sydney came under suspicion in the hunt for a possible Fenian 'cell'. Patrick Connery was now seventy but, while his name does not appear among those who contributed to the Sydney *Freeman's Journal's* Irish Prisoners Fund in 1866, it is very likely that he came to the attention of the police not least because of his troubled relationship with Simeon Henry Pearce.

They found no Fenians in New South Wales. Moreover O'Farrell, in his last confession, denied he was a member of the organisation and claimed to have acted alone. Recent historical research has uncovered little to prove otherwise. Patrick O'Farrell has argued convincingly that 'Fenianism was too strong a meat for the average Irish-Australian stomach',[15] and while Amos had identified certain Fenian sympathies among recent Irish arrivals, this seemed always to have stopped short of action. It is quite possible that Patrick Connery had some regard for the Fenians, but their nationalism would have been insufficient for the Connery preoccupation had always been with the robbery of the poor by the rich in Ireland.

The New South Wales Government fell on 13 October, its passing hastened by the refusal of Westminster to submit the Treason-Felony Act for the royal assent. A Committee of Inquiry under the new administration found 'no Fenian Conspiracy had ever existed in the colony', but a wily

Parkes managed to have this result set aside.[16] The whole affair served as a stark reminder that for Irish Catholics in New South Wales little had changed.

Patrick Connery spent his final years in Randwick, in a house off Orange St.[17] He was only a short distance from Blenheim House, but by then it occupant felt more secure. Pearce had regarded the granting of a municipal council to Randwick in 1859 as a personal triumph, embellished by his terms spent as mayor. Moreover, he had prospered in property speculation. Thus Pearce's Randwick had been achieved and now no old Irishman could alter it character.

Patrick Connery was eighty one years of age when the last of the Irish agrarian rebels appeared in North Eastern Victoria. Just like the Connerys in the 1830s, Ned Kelly and his gang are men out of their time, involved in a hopeless struggle. The events take place in Australia, but it could easily be Ireland, under a warm sun.

Ned, James and Dan Kelly's Ireland is that which their parents left, well before the Famine. In particular, it is the Ireland of Tipperary, notorious for agrarian violence. Their father John, from Moyglass, was convicted for stealing two pigs, at Cashel, in 1841 and was transported for seven years to Van Diemen's Land[18] to 'pine [his] young [life] away in starvation and misery among tyrants worse than the promised hell itself'.[19] His family grew up in a North Eastern Victoria where the limits of the Australian frontier had been reached. This produced the 'extreme rural poverty, anger and frustration which was the context of the famous Kelly outbreak'.[20]

Ellen Quinn, from Armoy, County Antrim, had been of the better class of life, but as a widow on a small selection with no capital could do little for her large family. Her three sons attempted to stave off the antipodean equivalent of the *spailpín fánach* future through horses, but the line between dealing and stealing was often imprecise. Their involvement in the equine trade inevitably led to conflict with the police, which culminated in a bitter clash at Stringybark Creek on 28 October 1878 and the deaths of three Irish policemen.

Respectable Victorian society was shocked and outraged. The Governor outlawed Ned, Dan (James was in prison since 1877)[21] and their two unidentified companions, later named as Steve Hart and Joseph Byrne, on 15 November.[22] Members of the public were now free to shoot them on sight. However, Ned and his gang proved elusive as the forces of law and order encountered widespread ambivalence in North Eastern Victoria, not to mention outright support for the outlaws. This increased when Ned Kelly embraced the mantle of an Irish agrarian rebel determined to destroy an unjust system and fused it with the daring of an Australian bushranger. A spectacular hold-up of the town of Euroa, on 9 December, was followed by that of Jerilderie, just across the border in New South Wales, on 8 February 1879. Here Edward Kelly left his famous letter which not alone defends his own actions but recounts the suffering and oppression of the Irish at home and their terrible treatment as convicts in Australia. Moreover, he identified a common cause: 'but there was never such a thing as justice in the English laws but any amount of injustice to be had',[23] and thereby invoked the Whiteboys, Caravats and, ultimately, the Connerys.

If Patrick Connery had not enough to see parallels with events in his own life, there was the matter of the liberal Attorney-General of Victoria. Sir Bryan O'Loghlen was Michael's son not to mention M.P. for Clare. Indeed, on 27 December 1878 the first law officer became acting premier and assumed responsibility for the pursuit of the Kellys.[24] In his youth he had been involved with Young Ireland, but the gap between him and Ned Kelly was as great as that which separated the Connerys from his father.

After Jerilderie, the £4,000 offered by Victoria for the apprehension of the Kelly gang was matched by New South Wales, but the four horsemen had vanished. Had they escaped to America or perished in the bush? Patrick Connery never learned their fate.

The last of the Connerys was eighty three when he died on 24 May 1880. His nephew James made the funeral arrangements, but there was no death notice in the *Sydney Morning Herald*. Patrick was buried in a single grave, in the Catholic Section of Rookwood Cemetery on 26 May. There is no headstone.[25]

Patrick Connery witnessed the last great articulation of a tradition stretching back to the Caravats and the Whiteboys. It was soon extinguished, after his death, as Dan Kelly, Joe Byrne and Steve Hart all perished in a clash with the Victorian Police at Glenrowan and Ned was hanged by the courts. Yet, like the Connerys in Irish folklore and song, the manner of their failure has influenced Australian literature, cinema and painting.

Ellen English Connery died at her daughter's residence in Smithfield on 12 February 1886. She left an estate of £1001 and is buried in the Church of England Cemetery. Her son James, a very successful butcher, died at Newtown on 16 February 1912. He left no will and the estate was valued at £1,606 12s 03d. James is buried with his wife's people, the Urquharts, in Waverley Cemetery not too far from the Irish 1798 Memorial. Mary Connery Dummett died on 2 June 1919 and joined her mother in the Church of England Cemetery. Both James and Mary had large families so there is no shortage of the descendants of John Connery and Ellen English in New South Wales.

James, son of John Connery and Ellen English.

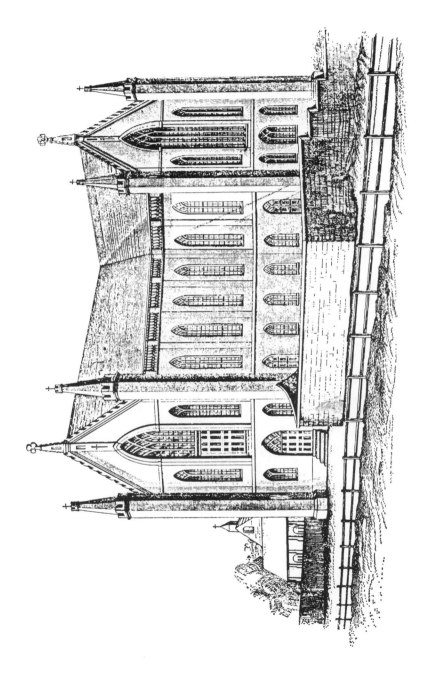

J Fowler Delt.

St MARY'S CATHEDRAL.

Engd by Mansell.

102

Chapter 12

Epilogue

In vain will you seek traces of the Connerys in New South Wales. The Lachlan Swamp now forms part of Centennial Park, but there is no plaque to its former guardians. Sydney Cemetery is entombed beneath the Central Railway Station. In 1901, the remains of John and James, together with thousands of others, were removed to Bunnerong, to lie somewhere overlooking Botany Bay. Patrick still rests alone and unmarked, not far from the Catholic Mortuary Chapel, at Rookwood. The brothers no more than the 22,000 men and 5,000 women who were sent direct from Ireland to New South Wales are gone into the Australian Past.

The Connerys never achieved an antipodean prominence to match that of home. Therefore, their resurrection is almost solely dependent on surviving documents in the official repositories. Any folklore they may have engendered did not survive the rapidly changing, urban context of greater Sydney. Moreover, there is no family tradition among John's descendants to preserve an image of *na sárfhir* under southern skies.

The Connerys in New South Wales form part of that great enforced diaspora to the Australian continent, beginning with the *Queen* in 1791 and ending with the *Hougoumont* in 1868.[1] While *na sárfhir* never achieved a significant impact in their land of exile, neither did they fade into respectable obscurity. By recalling their lives as convicts and freemen it is hoped that a worthwhile dimension had been added to Australian historiography but more importantly that the Connerys have finally been brought home. The story of the Connerys covers eighty years of the nineteenth century. Their greatest significance is for that short period when they successfully opposed the forces of modernisation. Thereafter they were swept onwards by change. Although that Irish world which sustained the Connerys was destroyed by *An Gorta* yet it could echo from beyond the grave, even in the North Eastern Victoria of the 1870s. It is only by studying the Connerys that the power and breadth of the whole tradition of agrarian dissent can be appreciated.

If the Connerys were agrarian rebels and faction fighters, they were also Irish convicts in New South Wales. Their adaptation to the penal system was sufficient to ensure survival and, in the cases of John and Patrick at the Lachlan Swamp, a great deal of personal freedom. In studying the Connerys' enforced contribution to the colony's infrastructure, the input of 22,000 men and 5,000 women is recalled and highlighted. Yet, both as convicts and freemen, incidents occur which evoke memories of other days and demonstrate that their lives in New South Wales will not serve merely as typical case studies.

Finally, it is the interest in traditional Irish music which has ensured the Connerys' survival into modern times. This book has attempted to restore the historical context such that the mention of *Na Conairigh* will invoke powerful images of Ireland and New South Wales in the nineteenth century.

MUINNTIR CONNICRE.

1. A Cuimín mall-aig-te guióim-re veac-air ort, — ag-ur grá-in Mic
2. 'Té béaó na fear-am ann ir véan faó mact-nam ar — á-r gcú-ir vá
3. Tá jaic-éió gai-r-io vá véanaó ó maio-in vú-inn, ag-ur trú-ir vá
4. A bainriogan bean-nuig-te, ra Rí na bflai-teas geal, tab-air fuar-cailt orrainn

Dé, Ar an gar-ar úo tá — ceangail-te go
pléió, Ó-vo rear-uig rí ó'na react ar mai-vin go vcí tar
réip: Culaio fair-rai-ge, níó nár caic-ea-mar i
arson Ir ar an mban-art-la tá rambai-l-e go

vlúc leo' taob. Ir iao vo vear-b-ui-g
é-ir a naoi. Do crit an tal-am fúinn le
vcú-ir ár raogail. M.arat feabar ár gear-aio vúinn bí ár
vúb-ac 'n ár nvéió. Le linn an ai-r(e)-pi-nn

na leab-ar-tá go hú-mal 'ra mbréag, Do cuir na
linn na leab-ar-tá vá vcab-airt 'ra mbréag, Mo greió an
muin-il cnag-aig-te go voim-in 'ran ao-l, nó gur
bí-vió'g ag-all-am, 'rag guin-e cum Dé, Ar na

Con-ner-ys tar na fair-ri-gib go vcír na New South Wales
t-an-am boct, tá re vam-an-ta, má'r ri-or vo'n cléir
car-aó rinn cumtéar-mai caic-eam i-n rna New South Wales
Con-ner-ys a tabairt a-bail-e cug-ainn ó rna New South Wales

Appendix I

The Connery songs

1. Na Connerys (Breathnach 1920*)
   A Chomthain mhallaithe guímse deacair ort a' s gráin Mhic Dé,
   A' s ar an ngasra úd 'tá ceangailte go dlúth led' thaobh,
   Mar sibh do dhearbhaigh i láthair Choisdealaigh ar 'n triúr fear séimh
   'S a chuir na Connerys thar na farigí 'dtí 's na New South Wales.

   An té bheadh 'na seasamh ann 'sa dhéanfadh machnamh ar ár gcúis
   da phlé,
   Mar do sheasaigh sí ón a seacht ar maidin go dtí tar éis a naoi,
   Chrith an talamh fúinn le linn na leabhartha agá dtabhairt sa mbréig,
   A's mo ghraidin-se an t-anam bocht tá sé damanta nó is fíor í an chlé!

   Tá jacéid gairid 'á dheanamh ó mhaidin dúinn a's triús dó réir,
   Culaithe farraigí ní nár thaithigheamar i dtúis ár saoil,
   Muireach feabhas ár gcaradais bhí ár muiníl cnagtha is sin go
   doimhinn san aol,
   Nó gur casadh sinn chun tearmaí caitheamh is na New South Wales.

   A Bhanrion bheannaithe, sa Rí na bhFlathas geal tabhair fuasgailt
   orainn araon,
   A's ar an mbanartla atá sa mbaile go dubhach 'nár ndéidh,
   Le linn an Aifrinn bígí ag agallamh a's ag guidhe chun Dé,
   Ar na Connerys a thabhairt abhaile chugainn os na New South Wales

   Translation (Daniel Kiely, 1987)
   1
   Oh *Chomthain* I wish misery to you and the wrought of the Lord
   As well as to your associates who stood by your word
   It was you who produced evidence, fabricated tales
   That sent the Connerys over the ocean to New South Wales.

2

Observers in court interested in our fate
Would be present from early morning till evening late;
The earth tremored when false evidence was admitted to court
May the scoundrel who damned his soul get his just reward!

3

We are being fitted with short jackets and trousers to match,
Seafaring clothing our style do not match
But for a friend's intervention we were hanged and buried in lime
With no term of incarceration in a foreign clime.

4

Oh blessed King and Queen of heaven have pity on our plight
And on our sorrowing mother at home tonight;
Think of us at Masses and in your prayers
That God will send the Connerys home again from New South Wales.

* Pádraig Breathnach, *Ár gCeól Féinig,* pp. 144-5
Similar versions are to be found as:
(a) Na Conairigh (Ó Cadhla, 1922) in *Eachtradh Eibhlís i dTír na nlongantas.*
(b) Muintir Chonaire (Micil Shile, 1902) in M. Ní Annagáin and S. de Chlainndiolúin (eds.), *'Londubh an Chairn'* Being Songs of the Irish Gaels in staff and sol-fa With English Metrical Translations, (London, 1927), pp. 16, 33, 34, (see facsimile of musical arrangement, p. 105).
(c) Na Connerys (Seán Ó Laighin, 1940) in Liam de Noraidh, *Ceol ón Mumháin,* (Dublin, 1965) p. 42.
(d) Na Connerys in Liam Ó Murchú, *Na Connerys dráma trí ghníomh,* (Dublin, 1974).
(e) Na Connerys (Mhicilín Shile) in N. Tóibín, *Duanaire Déiseach.*
(f) Na Connerys in T. Ó Concheanainn, *Nua-Dhuanaire Cuid III,* (Dublin, 1978), p. 85 (edited reprint of Breathnach).
(g) Na Connerys in J. Crowley, *Jimmy Crowley's Irish Song Book With Music and Guitar Chords,* (Cork, 1986), p. 89.

2. Na Conairigh (Uí Choinghealla, in Ó Milléadha,1936)
Na Conairigh na sárfhir is iad atáim a áireamh,
A cuireadh uainn thar sáile isna ráigiúin i gcéin;
Is danaid dúinne uainn iad san áit ná faighidh siad fuascailt,
Is sinn anso faoi bhuaireamh i mBoth a' Dúin na gcraobh.

Sé a dtigh a bhíodh go buachach, go fáidhiuil, fáiltiuil, fuarmach,
Gheal-chupordach, mo bhuaireamh, fá mhór-chuid bhfeóil.
Lucht taistil cnoc is sléibhte agus straigiléirí aonair,
Bheadh a leaba agus a mbéile agus féile 'n-a gcóir.

Chuadar go Portláirge a d'iarraidh dul thar sáile;
Sin ní ná raibh i ndán dóibh, 's níor ránaigh sé dóibh;
Mar bhí fear a mbraithe i láthair, thug timpeall orthu an gárda,
Is isteach arís a sáthadh iad i n-áras faoi bhrón.

Tugadh iad súd láithreach go príosún mór Phortláirge,
An t-áras daingean láidir úd, gan fagháil ar dul 'na gaor,
Ach thugadar a sála dos na fallaí móra árda,
'S an tSiúir amach gur shnámhadar gan spleáchas do'n seighléir

Mo mhallacht ort is léir ort, a rascail bhradaigh bhréaghaigh!
Nára fada an lá go n-éagfair gan bhaochas Mhic Dé;
Is tú ghlac an bhreab go h-éasca is a dhearbhaigh an t-éitheach,
A chuir na Conairigh thar tréan-mhuir ó Bhoth a' Dúin na gcraobh.

Translation (Daniel Kiely, 1987)
It is of the Connerys, those staunch men that I do relate,
Transported across the Ocean to a penal state;
We sorely miss them from us in a place of no reprieve
As here in leafy Bohadoon we lament and grieve.

Their homestead neat and tidy oozed welcome from within,
Bright cupboarded, I ween* with lashings of food;
The travellers of hill and mountain and the lonely vagrant found therein
A welcome to a bed and the fare was good.

They travelled down to Waterford intending emigration
But that was not to be and their plans misfired.
A traitor present, spotting them passed on the information
And in barracks once again were in sadness confined.

Now Waterford Prison was their immediate destination
A formidable structure from where none could hope to flee.
But they scaled the prison walls with fierce determination
Swam the River Suir and once again were free.

A curse be upon you lying thieving traitor.
May the day soon come when you die without God's grace,
You took the bribe confirming your false favour
And sent the Connerys for ever from Bohadoon *na gcraobh.*

* Old Munster English roughly equivalent to ... to fancy or ... to recall.
An edited reprint of Na Conairigh can be found in Ó Concheanainn,
Nua-Dhuanaire Cuid III, pp. 28-9.

3.   Na Connerys (Shéamais Mhailldí, in Tóibín, 1978)
     Inseoidh mise scéal dhaoibh más é bhur dtoil liom éisteacht,
     Ag tagairt do na séimhfhir atá sealad uainn ar fán;
     Gur tógadh iad go gléasta le scoil agus le léamh iad,
     Le clú, le meas, le héifeacht is le haonghean dá gcáil.
     Da siúlfainn tír na hÉireann, Sasana le chéile,
     Alba, Van Diemen, an Éigipt is an Spáinn,
     Is geallaimse gan bhréag daoibh nach raghadh ag insint éithigh,
     Nach bhfaighinn a neart ná a dtréineacht in aon bheirt deartháir.

     Is iad na Conairigh na sárfhir, is iad atáim a áireamh,
     Cé go bhfuilid seal ar fán uainn in áras faoi bhrón,
     Is í a gcistin a bhíodh go buacach, go fearúil, flaithiúil, fairsing,
     Gealchupordach, gealsuáilceach, faoi mhórchuid den fheoil.
     Dá gcastaí bochta Dé ann nó taistealaí bocht aonair
     Bhíodh a leaba agus a mbéile agus gach féile acu le fáil.
     Anois tá na madraí go craosach á cartadh ó gach taobh ann,
     Sin cosc ó Dhia ar aoinne ar mhéin leis ní a fháil.

     Bhíodh an saighdear milis, láidir á riar i dteách na sárfhear;
     Bhíodh an Eaglais gach féile ar staeision go hard;
     Ach anois ó tá na tréanfhir le crosa is falsaí an tsaoil seo
     Faoi tharcaisne ag meirligh is á n-éileamh gach lá.
     Tógadh iad go buachach, gan achrann, gan chruatan,
     Go súgach, sultmhar, suáilceach, gan bhuaireamh, gan ghá;
     Bhí cabhair is cúnamh Dé acu, bhí buíochas óg is aosta acu,
     Is ba mhaith an ceart gan aon locht a bheith ar a mhéin nó ar a gcáil.

     Is a Dhia, nacht bocht an scéal é á chur ar fud na hÉireann
     Ag grathain ghránna an Bhéarla nár ghéill riamh don Pháis;
     Is go bhfuil 'fhios ag gach aoinne nach rabhadar ciontach riamh in aon
     choir,
     Ach ag seasamh 'na gceart féineach is gan é acu le fáil.

Chuadar go Port Láirge ag iarraidh dul thar sáile,
Siúd ní ná raibh i ndán dóibh is ní tharla sé ina gcomhair.
Bhí fear an bhraite láimh leo thug timpeall orthu an garda,
Is isteach arís gur sádh iad in áras faoi bhrón.

Nuair a chuala na meirligh go raibh greim acu ar na sárfhir,
Go deimhin ba mhór an phrae leo iad a thraochadh le cnáib,
Crochadh nó transporting amach ar fad thar bóchna,
I bhfad ó ghaol is ó chóngas gan fóirthint go brách.
Tá an bhaintreach go brónach is a dílleachtaí le deora,
Nuair a cuireadh na hógfhir thar a n-eolas chun fáin,
Thugadh prátaí, im is feoil dóibh 's an tine dheargmhóna,
Is an fuacht, go deimhin, ba dhóigh liom nár bháol doibh a fháil.

Seachas Judas gránna an chlampair a chuir Íosa Críost i dteannta,
Nárbh ina chroí istigh a bhí an feall is b'fhalsa í a phóg!
Is gurbh é a chloisim ag an seanracht go bhfuil a anam siúd i dteannta
In Ifreann gan amhras is é go cantalach á dhó.
Má thagann sé chun críche' dóibh go bhfeicfeam arís iad,
A bpardún glán ón Rí acu is iad á insint dúinn faoi shó,
Cruinneoimid ina dtimpeall gan spleáchas do na peelers,
Is beidh ár gcornán dí againn go haoibhinn á ól.

Ar chuala sibh, a dhaoine, an plean a cheap an dís úd,
Go raibh an scéal ag gabháil timpeall nó gur chríochnaíodar a ngnó,
Gur bhailíodar na sála thar na geataí móra arda,
Is amach ansiúd go brách leo gan spleáchas dá namhaid?
Beidh againn glór na píbe, ceol, spórt is aoibhneas
Ó mhaidin go dtí an óiche is ón óiche go dtí an lá.
Beidh na bairillí ar a bhfaobhar againn is sinn ag fáscadh lámh a chéile
Agus sláinte gheal na hÉireann ní thaoscfaimid go brách.

Translation (Daniel Kiely, 1987)
I have a story to tell, pray listen to me,
Concerning brave men who have now crossed the sea;
They were reared in style with reading and writing,
Well honoured, esteemed with all true traits uniting.
If you travelled all Ireland and England as well,
Spain, Egypt, Scotland and more could I tell
That nowhere could you find without falsehood or lies
The power and strength of those two brave boys.

It is of the Connerys those staunch men that I do relate,
Now imprisoned for a time in a far away state
Their household was comfortable, inviting, generous,
Well cupboarded, pleasant with a good supply of eatables.
Welcome was the poor beggar or the lonely outcast stray
Sure of a bed and meal to cheer them on their way
Now scavenging dogs swarm around the domain
Discouraging those who were wont to remain.

This used be a home of good cheer with potent cider aplenty
*Its inhabitants church going, religious, with a deep degree of piety,
But now subdued by falsehoods and bearing fearful crosses,
Reminded daily of their fate and their generous losses,
Their rearing was honourable without strife or privation,
Joyful, pleasant, playful without need or desperation;
God gave them grace and blessing for young and old to cherish,
They were straightforward without fault of character without blemish.

Oh God what a grim story is being circulated in the land
By the nasty English hirelings a compromise band;
*The Connerys were above reproach the people say,
*Fighting for their rights without any hope today.
They travelled down to Waterford intending emigration
But that was not to be and their plans misfired.
A traitor present spotting them passed on the information
And in barracks once again were in sadness confined.

When the news spread around that our heroes were taken,
The Law was determined to have its say,
Hanging or transportation without solace or haven
Far away from home and friends for ever and a day.
The women folk are moaning and the children in tears
Since our heroes were transported to foreign parts unknown,
Of famine cold or hardship they had no need to fear
Since the hospitable bonds of friendship from childhood were sown.

Just like Judas the traitor who betrayed Our Lord Jesus
With wickedness of heart and a falsifying kiss!
Those scoundrels too when they are taken from us
May in Hell fire burn, tormented is our wish.
Should the day ever dawn that we again see them
Granted King's pardon and living in peace,
Without spies or peelers, we'll gladly surround them
And toast to their health and their life a new lease.

There is a rumour circulating of a plan to aid escaping
So the story goes that their efforts bear fruit,
They scaled the prison wall and to freedom bravely leaping,
Away from spies and enemies is forever their lot.
We'll celebrate with music with sport and with pleasure
From morning till night and again from dusk until dawn.
We'll drink and rejoice the whole time at our leisure
And toast our dear old Ireland again and again.

* denotes lines where a more literal English translation has been used in the text.

Similar versions are to be found as

(a) Na Conairí (Pádraig Barún, 1920), in Labhrás Ó Cadhla, (Béaloideas 1936), Department of Irish Folklore U.C.D., MS 289, pp. 102-6 (three brothers version)

(b) Na Conairí (Seán Ó Caoimh, 1925), in *An Sguab,* June 1925, pp. 376-7 (ditto).

(c) Na Conneries (Nioclás, sean-nós, Tóibín), in N. Tóibín L.P., Gael Linn, 1977, CEF. 062 (two brothers version).

Table 1 — Land Distribution in Civil Parishes of Kilgobinet, Seskinane, Colligan and Lickoran as depicted in Tithe Applotment 1827-34.

ACRE SIZE		0-5	5-15	15-30	30-50	50-70	70-90	90-120	120-150	150-200	200→
KILGOBINET	HOLDINGS A 113	—	8	7	8	10	16	10	4	4	19
	HOLDINGS B 106	—	15	21	17	7	16	13	6	3	14
SESKINANE	HOLDINGS A 197	6	12	33	51	37	12	23	7	5	11
	HOLDINGS B 187	5	11	35	51	37	11	25	6	4	2
COLLIGAN	HOLDINGS A 22	—	—	2	2	2	3	3	2	2	6
	HOLDINGS B 18	—	—	2	3	4	2	2	2	1	2
LICKORAN	HOLDINGS A 48	9	5	19	5	3	1	—	1	3	2
	HOLDINGS B 43	9	5	17	5	3	1	—	1	2	—

Note:

(i) Holdings A are actual holdings as extracted directly from Tithe Applotment Books. Holdings B are obtained by excluding head landlords and arbitrarily dividing up joint holdings. As no information on landowners is included in the Lickoran Tithe Applotment, head landlord holdings were designated on the basis of information gained about the occupants elsewhere.

(ii) While about 5,000 of Kilgobinet's 16,134 acres were mountain (bog not given), one half of Seskinane's 17,030 acres was comprised of mountain and bog. Colligan's 3,679 acres only contained 30 acres in bog (no mountains). *Poor Inquiry, Appendix F*, p. 297. Lickoran was consolidated in Modeligo insufficient information given to disentangle it.

(iii) Seskinane had 200 actual holdings but as three of these were double holdings within a single townland, they have been consolidated and the number reduced to 197.

113

Appendix II

Land holding in Sliabh gCua

Joint tenancy was significant only in Kilgobinet where it accounted for 22 of the 87 holdings, spread over ten of the 23 townlands, Barracree, Ballyconnery, Bohadoon, Coolnasmear, Kilgobinet, Kilnafrehane, Ballyknock, Glidane (sic), Monarud, and Deelish, on various estates; the family connection is obvious only on eight of the holdings. The remainder which are unclear includes the jointholding of Mary Lynch and Patrick Connery in Bohadoon. If the direct holdings of head landlords are excluded and joint tenancies split up equally between their partners we can approximate the real farm structure within the parish. As most of the land reserved by landlord is mountain except in the case of the townland of Scart, the equal split presents our only troublesome assumption. We now have 106 holdings of which 14 per cent (15) are less than 15 acres, 20 per cent (21) between 15 and 30 acres and 16 per cent (17) between 30 and 50 acres. Please see Table 1.

Thus 50 per cent of all holdings fall below 50 acres with particular concentrations of small farmers in the townlands of Bohadoon, Kilgobinet and Monarud. The tithe valuation of each holding, with six classes stretching from first quality land to mountain, capture the variety of soil quality within each plot and provides a more real value of each farm. If an adjusted acreage measure is adopted it may be that 50 acres is too conservative a cut off point for a definition of a small farmer. At the apex of the social scale we have 14 holdings exceeding 200 acres, in three of these whole townlands are consolidated. Barracree had joint tenants but in Currabaha and Tallowcoole (more) there is only the one landholder. Perhaps middlemen are to be found in this category.

Unlike Kilgobinet, the absence of the fifth and sixth class tithe valuation reflect the better soils of the civil parish of Colligan. If the direct holdings of the head landlords, which accounted for 5 of the 22 holdings, are again excluded, a dominance of medium (50 to 90 acres) and large (90 acres and over) farmers is obvious. In contrast the civil parish of Seskinane places us firmly back again in the Comeragh-Monavullagh uplands and foothills. By excluding the holdings of head landlords (15) and arbitrarily dividing joint tenancies (5); 197 holdings are reduced to 187. A slightly higher proportion 55 per cent (102) are less than 50 acres than in Kilgobinet and a particular concentration of small farmers are found in 5 of the 28 townlands/denominations i.e. Blantisore (sic), Scaheens (sic), Knockboy, Cahernaleague, and Mountook (sic). Holdings of less than five acres comprise 3 per cent (5) of the total, between 5 and 15 acre 6 per cent (11), 15 to 30 acres made up 19 per cent (35) and 30 to 50 acres accounted for the final 27 per cent (51). Unlike Kilgobinet there are only two holdings greater than 200 acres, a possible explanation suggests itself in the relative presence of medium farmers in the two parishes. In the categories 50 to 70 acres and 70 to 90 acres Seskinane has 26 per cent of its holdings Kilgobinet 22 per cent moreover less than a quarter of Seskinane's medium farmers are found in the second category.

Finally, the civil parish of Lickoran contained the greatest proportion of small holdings. In the townland of Lyreattin (25 holdings) alone no farm exceeded 40 acres.

NOTES

Chapter 1

1. *Waterford Chronicle*, 23 July 1838.
2. The common law of the Irish peasant community invariably in conflict with that embodied in the statutes which had to be imposed from outside and were, therefore, unable to command any moral authority. This feature was shared by European peasant society which was bedevilled from the 14th century to the 18th century by such legal conflicts. E.P. Thompson, 'The Moral Economy of the English Crowd in the Eighteenth Century', *Past and Present*, no. 50, (February, 1971), pp. 76-136, has treated the phenomenon at length. The enforcers of Irish peasant law as J. Lee, 'The Ribbonmen', in T.D. Williams (ed), *Secret Societies in Ireland* (Dublin, 1973), p. 32, has pointed out, were extremely levelheaded and practical: 'They shared few of the illusions of European peasant rebels from the Atlantic to the Urals that the "good king" was on their side'.
3. 'Na Connerys' (Shéamais Mhailldí), in N. Tóibín, *Duanaire Déiseach* (Dublin, 1978), p. 29 [hereafter Tóibín, *Song 3*].
4. *Poor Inquiry: Appendix F*, 38, H.C. 1836, XXXIII, I, p. 121 [hereafter *Poor Inquiry Appendix F*].
5. J.S. Donnelly Jr., *The Land and the People of Nineteenth-Century Cork, The Rural Economy and the Land Question* (London and Boston, 1975), p. 55 [herafter Donnelly, *Land and People of Cork*].
6. M. Beames, *Peasants and Power: Whiteboy Movements and Their Control in Pre-Famine Ireland* (Brighton and New York, 1983), [hereafter Beames, *Peasant and Power*].
7. See Lee, op. cit., p. 32.
8. *Waterford Chronicle*, 23 July 1838.
9. Tóibín, *Song 3*, p. 28 (two brothers song)
10. *Waterford Mail*, 22 August 1835.
11. *Waterford Mirror*, 31 March 1838.
12. *Waterford Chronicle*, 23 July 1835.
13. *Waterford Mail*, 6 August 1834.
14. Three denominations of Bohadoon; North, South and Bohadoon Mountain are contained in *Ordnance Survey*, Waterford, 1841, sheets 22-3.
15. See J. Burtchaell, '19th Century Society in County Waterford' in *Decies* No. XXX (Autumn, 1985), pp. 25-34.; 'A Typology of Settlement and Society in County Waterford c 1850' in Nolan, W., and Power, T. P., (eds), *Waterford History & Society* (Dublin, 1992), pp. 541-78.
16. See also An t-Athair Colmcille, O.C.S.O., 'Where was Sliabh gCua?' in *Decies* No. 46 (Autumn, 1992), pp. 5-9.
17. T. Ó Flannghaile (ed), *Eachtra Ghiolla an Amaráin or the Adventures of a Luckless Fellow and other poems by Donnchadh Ruadh Mac Conmara with Life of the Poet by the late John Fleming* (Dublin, 1887), pp. 50-1.
18. Ó Flannghaile, op. cit., p. 4.
19. Ibid., pp. 4-5.
20. Letter from William, Bishop of Waterford and Lismore, on acts of violence committed within his diocese during 1786, with supporting testimony from clergy, 14 February 1787, N.L.I., Bolton MS 16350, fols. 89-92.
21. Despite an oral tradition (see p. 5) which maintains that all the brothers received an education, only John is returned as having one in the Convict Records of New South Wales. In 1841, 71% of the population of Co. Waterford was returned as being unable

116

to either read or write English, the third worse literacy rate in all of Ireland – only Galway and Mayo were worse. *Census Ire.*, 1841 504, H.C. 1843, XXIV, I, p. XXXII.

22. C. Smith, *The Present and Ancient State of the County of Waterford* (Dublin, 1746), p. 34.

23. T. Fitzpatrick, *Waterford during the Civil War, 1641-53* (Waterford, 1912), pp. 42, 57.

24. Name spelled as Connory and O'Connory: S. Pender (ed), *Census of Ireland, 1659: A Census of Ireland circa 1659 with supplementary material from the Poll Money ordinances (1660-1661)* (Dublin, 1942), p. 337.

25. Pedigree of O'Conry of Dungarvan, Co. Waterford and Seville, Spain c. 1650-1780, Genealogical Office, MS 164, fols. 64-5.

26. Tóibín, *Song* 3, p. 28.

27. Tithe Applotment Parish of Kilgobinet, N.A., T.A.B., 29/23 1829, no. 47.

28. *Waterford Chronicle*, 23 July 1835.

29. The estate consisted of lands in counties Waterford and Limerick. It was sold in 1839 as comprising 6,474 acres of *fertile* land. The county Waterford portion, which was the largest, ran to about 6,000 acres when mountain and marginal land was included. As well as Bohadoon the Holmes Estate held Coolnasmear, Kilgobinet, Knockaunagloon, Ballyneety and Kiladangan. It also held Ballycondon, Castle Mills, Killea and Rhincrew Abbey close to the town of Youghal. The county Limerick part of the estate was based on the town of Kilmallock. See *Waterford Mail,* 2 March 1839, 24 April 1839; *Limerick Chronicle,* 20 April 1839.

30. See Appendix II, Land Holding in Sliabh gCua.

31. *Poor Inquiry, Appendix F,* pp. 192-3.

32. See D. Mahony to Major W. Miller, 21 April 1831, N.A., O.P., M. 47/1831; *Waterford Mirror,* 20 April 1831, 23 April 1831, 14 March 1835; *Waterford Mail,* 23 April 1831, 14 March 1835.

33. P. Ó Milléadha (ed), 'Seanchas Sliabh gCua', *Béaloideas,* vol. VI, 1936, pp. 182-4 [herafter Seanchas Sliabh gCua].

34. Beames, *Peasants and Power,* pp. 88, 99, 101.

35. *Waterford Mirror,* 30 April 1831.

Chapter 2

1. Lee, op. cit., pp. 27-8.

2. *Clonmel Advertiser, Waterford Chronicle,* 23 October 1834.

3. N.A., O.P., M. 64/1830, M. 109/1831, 1936/1832 (October), 29/34/1835, 29/85/1836, 29/32/1837, 29/65/1838; C.S.O.R.P., 2723/1831; *Waterford Mail,* 9 March 1833.

4. M. B. Kiely and W. Nolan 'Politics, Land and Rural Conflict in County Waterford c. 1830-1845' in *Waterford History & Society,* pp. 459-94.

5. P.E.W. Roberts, 'Caravats and Shanvests: Whiteboyism and Faction Fighting in East Munster, 1802 – 1811', in S. Clarke and J.S. Donnelly Jr. (eds.), *Irish Peasants Violence and Political Unrest 1780– 1914* (Manchester and Madison, 1983), pp. 66-7.

6. Ibid., p. 74.

7. Ibid., pp. 73-7.

8. *Poor Inquiry,* Appendix F, p. 28.

9. See below, pp. 20-1.

10. A Mr. Murphy put the whole faction problem in context at an anti-tithe meeting in Kilmacthomas in August 1832. 'Their conduct was opposed to the advice of Mr. O'Connell; and who was the man that loved Ireland better that he did ... While the friends of Ireland were struggling for her regeneration deluded men were bringing

ruin on themselves and misery on the whole country'. Murphy advised the people to urge the Poleens and Gows to reform however if they persisted 'to give them up to the hands of offended justice'. *Waterford Chronicle*, 14 August 1832.

11. See pp. 13, 18; Fr. Condon, P.P., invoked the ultimate sanction and threatened to withhold the last rites and close up the chapel of Rathcormack but to no effect. (*Waterford Chronicle*, 3 October 1835).

12. This group included Thomas Wyse, merchant/landowner of Waterford city; the largest Catholic landowners, the Barrons, in particular Henry Winston, Pierce George and Philip, the Dungarvan merchants John Mathew Galwey, Andrew Carbery and John Dower; and Dominick Ronayne, barrister of Ardsallagh. In the 1826 election they also had the enthusiastic support of Bishop Kelly of Waterford and Lismore, plus the catalyst of Daniel O'Connell as Stuart's election agent. Stuart and Sir Richard Musgrave of Tourin made up the Liberal Protestant component. Wyse, H.W. Barron, Ronayne and Musgrave became M.P.s in the 1830s.

13. D. McCartney, 'Electoral Politics in Waterford in the early 19th century' *Decies*, no. XX, (May, 1982), p. 49.

14. *Waterford Mail*, 16 February 1833.

15. This meeting was convened by H. Villiers Stuart. *Waterford Chronicle*, 26 February 1833.

16. Sub-Inspector Samuel Croker to Miller, 5 October 1833, N.A., O.P., 766/1833.

17. *Waterford Chronicle*, 5 October 1832; N.A., O.P., 1936/1832 (October).

18. Patrick Crehane (sic) manslaughter trial. *Waterford Chronicle*, 8 March 1834; ibid., P. Currane (sic), *Waterford Mirror*, 8 March 1834; F. Crossley to Miller, 19 October 1833, N.A., O.P., 766/1833.

19. *Waterford Mail*, 8 March 1834.

20. Croker to Miller, 18 October 1833, N.A., O.P., 766/1833. The town was experiencing a severe economic decline brought on by the general agricultural distress and complimented by industrial contraction. H.D. Inglis, *A Journey throughout Ireland during Spring, Summer, and Autumn, 1834* (London, 1835), vol. I, p. 72; Roberts, op. cit., p. 76 has already noted the popularity of Caravatism with the Carrick boatmen and textile workers.

21. *Waterford Chronicle*, 24 October 1833.

22. Crossley to Miller, 28 October 1833, N.A., O.P., 766/1833.

23. *Waterford Mirror*, 27 November 1833; *Waterford Chronicle*, 28 November 1833.

24. N.A., C.S.O.R.P., 5643/1833.

Chapter 3

1. *Waterford Chronicle*, 6 March 1834. William Power of Graigavalla (Rathgormack), one of the Gow leaders, stated at the trial he had gone to the fair to sell cattle and wheat. He had already lost three cows, when his cornhouse and stable were maliciously burnt with the police supposing Poleen involvement. N.A., O.P., 1936/1832 (February); *Waterford Mirror*, 3 March 1833. When the Power landholding (N.A., T.A.B., 29/9 1834) and the fact that 15 of those arrested in the Carrick affray were able to meet the onerous bail requirement is taken into account, it appears that the ambitious members of the middle class, which Roberts (op. cit., p. 86) states provided the leadership of the Caravats and Shanavests, were also to be found in their Poleen and Gow successors. This tends to contradict the convenient social evaluation of the *Waterford Chronicle* on 3 October 1833: 'They are the very dregs of the community – for the most part servant boys of the worst character, and a cowardly set when at all resisted'.

2. *Waterford Mail*, 8 March 1834.

3. Patrick Currane (sic) manslaughter trial, *Waterford Mirror*, 8 March 1834; Patrick Crehane (sic) manslaughter trial, *Waterford Chronicle*, 8 March 1834.

4. *Waterford Mirror*, op. cit.

5. G. de Beaumont, *Ireland: Social, Political and Religious*, W.C. Taylor (ed.), (London, 1839), vol. I, p. 328.

6. Foley was sub-sheriff for the County in 1826-7 and 1830-1 in which capacity he read the writ at the famous '26 election. It was on the sub-sheriff rather than the high sheriff, whose role was purely administrative and political, that fell the high risk function of supervising distraints and evictions.

7. Donnelly, *Land and People of Cork*, p. 68; Devon Commission: Evidence, pt. III, 657, H.C. 1845, XXI, I, Evid. 817.

8. M.R. Beames, 'Rural Conflict in Pre-Famine Ireland: Peasant Assasination in Tipperary 1837-1847', *Past and Present*, no. 81, (1978), p. 78.

9. *Waterford Chronicle*, 23 July 1835; *Waterford Mail*, 22 July 1835; *Waterford Mirror*, 25 July 1835.

10. Recapture of the Connerys – Interesting Particulars of their Extraordinary Escapes and Adventures, *Waterford Chronicle*, 31 March 1838 [hereafter Interesting Particulars].

11. *Waterford Chronicle*, 23 July 1835. A portion of Ballylemon woods was Foley's own property.

12. N.A., C.S.O.R.P., 6424/1833.

13. Crossley to Miller, 2 May 1834, N.A., O.P., 529/1834; *Waterford Chronicle*, 19 July 1834; N.A., O.P., 29/39 & 29/51/1837.

14. O'Keeffe, a Catholic, was an old man and extremely tough land distributor. He survived one assassination attempt but on 13 May 1838 he was shot while on his way to Mass and died later of his wounds.

15. *Waterford Chronicle*, 20 November 1834.

16. Seanchas Sliabh gCua, p. 183.

17. T. Foley to T. Drummond, 21 August 1835, & Statement of J. Bruce, 29 August 1835, N.A., C.S.O.R.P., 2743/1835; C.S.O.R.P., 1323/1835.

18. Trial of Jas and J. Connery, *Waterford Mail*, 14 March 1835; Trial of L. Crotty, *Waterford Mirror*, 14 March 1835. While Crotty was convicted of stating he did not see James strike Hackett with stones, the Connerys' trial suggests Crotty was implicating John.

19. It is likely that this was Thomas Foley's half brother William, a surgeon, and grandfather of the author Arthur Conan Doyle.

20. *Waterford Mirror*, ibid.

21. G. Prendergast to Lord Mulgrave, 10 July 1835, N.A., C.S.O.R.P., 2643/1835.

22. Resume of Fr. Prendergast's charges, *Waterford Chronicle*, 15 August 1835.

23. *Waterford Chronicle*, 28 April 1835.

24. Report on charges and findings, N.A., C.S.O.R.P., 2643/1835.

25. No. 21.

26. Bishop Abraham to Robert Power, foreman of Grand Jury, *Waterford Chronicle*, 6 August 1835.

27. *Waterford Chronicle*, 27 October 1835.

28. Ibid., 28 November 1835, 8 December 1835. Galwey's attempts, 1835-7, to wrest the borough of Dungarvan from the O'Connellite/Whig 'understanding' embodied in the Lichfield House Compact, further strained already poor relations. To do so he endeavoured to overcome, as he professed, undue clerical influence and to mobilise the poorest strata of the electorate, the fishermen, both extremely unpopular campaign options.

29. *Waterford Chronicle,* 1 November 1836.

30. Ibid., 23 July 1835.

31. Ibid.

32. Ibid.

33. Ibid.

34. Ibid.

35. N.A., O.P., 29/28 & 29/29/1835.

36. A. de Tocqueville, *Journeys to England and Ireland,* ed. by J.P. Mayer, trans. by G. Lawrence & K.P. Mayer (New Haven and London, 1958), p. 138.

37. De Beaumont, op. cit., vol. I, p. 299.

38. Edmond Power, of Ballygagin, Dungarvan, a United Irishman, is reputed to have said, while on the scaffold in 1799: *'Beidh lá eile ag an Paorach'* (Power will have another day). The phrase captured and tantalized popular imagination.

Chapter 4

1. Military correspondence, N.A., C.S.O.R.P., 2743/1835.

2. M. Jackson, Deposition, 28 August 1835, ibid.

3. Jackson claimed Bruce told him to open the door.

4. Foley to M. O'Loghlen, 3 October 1835, N.A., C.S.O.R.P., 2743/1835.

5. Foley to Drummond, 21 August 1835, ibid.

6. Foley to O'Loghlen, 3 October 1835, ibid.

7. W.S. Curry to Viscount Morpeth, 4 November 1835, ibid.

8. Editorial condemning J.M. Galwey, *Waterford Chronicle,* 2 May 1835.

9. M.A.G. Ó Tuathaigh, *Thomas Drummond and the Government of Ireland 1835-41* (O'Donnell Lecture N.U.I., 1977), no. 21, pp. 6-7.

10. *Evidence of Thomas Drummond, Esq., before the Select Committee of the House of Lords on the State of Ireland in respect of Crime* (Dublin, 1839), p. 146 [hereafter Evidence of Thomas Drummond].

11. Ó Tuathaigh, op. cit., p. 20.

12. R.B. O'Brien, *Coercion or Redress A Chapter from the Melbourne Administration With a Sketch of the Political Career of Thomas Drummond* (Manchester and London, 1881), p. 20.

13. No. 28, Chapter 3.

14. 125 copies were sent to T. Foley and F. Crossley on 24 November 1835.

15. Constable Hegarty had been redirected here by his informant.

16. Croker to Miller, 17 October 1835, N.A., C.S.O.R.P., 2743/1835.

17. Foley to O'Loghlen, 3 October 1835, ibid.

18. Curry to Morpeth, 4 November 1835, ibid.

19. N.A., O.P., 29/56/1835; *Waterford Chronicle,* 15 October 1835, 2 March 1836.

20. Kiely from Slievegrine also denied that there was any conspiracy to murder Mr. Walsh of Rockfield who was agent on the Ardmore estate where Kiely was a tenant in arrears of rent. According to the *Waterford Mail* of 23 March 1836, Kiely initially promised to name the conspirators if his life was spared but later claimed it was a mere pretext to avoid the rope. The *Mail* had a double murder theory in which the killing of Quinlan would be followed by that of Walsh. Morrissey via Fr. Dooley (*Waterford Chronicle,* 22 March 1836) did not believe there was such a conspiracy but if one was underway the participants were urged to desist as vengeance would follow.

21. Ibid.; *Waterford Mirror,* 21 March 1836.

22. S. Greany (sic), Information, 11 March 1836, N.A., C.S.O.R.P., 1557/1836; Unsigned minute, 9 January 1836, C.S.O.R.P., 2743/1835.

23. Drummond, 21 December 1835, N.A., C.S.O.R.P., 2743/1835.
24. Miller to Morpeth, 23 December 1835, ibid.
25. Drummond, 26 December 1835, ibid.
26. R. Purdey to Drummond, 20 May 1836, N.A., O.P., 78/1836.
27. Purdey to Drummond, 7 December 1835; Poster, N.A., O.P., 29/61/1835.
28. W. Lumsden to Miller, 6 December 1835, ibid.
29. R. Purdey to Drummond, 20 May 1836, N.A., O.P., 78/1836.
30. M. Singleton to Drummond, 6 June 1836, ibid.
31. Miller to Morpeth, 23 December 1835, N.A., C.S.O.R.P., 2743/1835.
32. Croker to Miller, 27 December 1835, ibid.
33. N.A., O.P., 29/1/8/1836.
34. Croker to Miller, 27 December 1835, op. cit.
35. Croker to Miller, 25 January 1836, N.A., O.P., 29/14/1836.
36. Sub-Constable T. Durham to Miller, 25 January 1836, ibid.
37. Statement of H. Bourke, ibid. It is presumed to mean that if the police can have a choice about dealing with robbers then the farmers can have a choice about supporting the police.
38. Ibid.
39. Miller to Drummond, 6 February 1836, ibid.
40. *Tipperary Constitution*, 8 March 1836.
41. See: W.P. Burke, *A History of Clonmel* (Waterford, 1907), pp. 361-405; M. Wall, 'The Whiteboys', in Williams, op. cit., pp. 13-25; J.S. Donnelly Jr., 'The Whiteboy Movement' in *Irish Historical Studies*, 21, no. 81, (1978), pp. 20-54.
42. Miller to Morpeth, 23 December 1835, op. cit.
43. Crossley to Miller, 14 February 1836, N.A., O.P., 29/14/1836.
44. Drummond, 16 February 1836, ibid.
45. Miller to Drummond, 15 February 1836, ibid.
46. Ibid.
47. The Connerys' itinerary is given as New Ross, England and America in Croker to Miller, 8 March 1836, N.A., C.S.O.R.P., 1332/1836.
48. *Waterford Chronicle*, 8 March 1836.
49. P. McGrath, Memorial, 28 November 1836, N.A., O.P., 29/86/1837.
50. Miller to H.W. Barron, 11 May 1836, N.A., O.P., 29/86/1837.
51. Bruce's reward of £10, the government reward of £50 and a sheriff's award of £40 mentioned in Miller to Morpeth, 23 December 1835, N.A., C.S.O.R.P., 2643/1835.
52. See Drummond to P. McGrath, 17 August 1836, N.A., C.S.O.R.P., 1332/1836. Also, O.P., 29/86/1837.
53. *Waterford Chronicle*, 10 March 1836; *Waterford Mail*, 12 March 1836.
54. N.A., O.P., 29/20/1836; *Tipperary Free Press*, 19 March 1836; *Clonmel Herald*, 23 July 1836.
55. Drummond, 8 March 1836, N.A., O.P., 29/20/1836.
56. N.A., C.S.O.R.P., 1557/1836; O.P., 78/1836.
57. Ibid.
58. *Waterford Mail*, 25 May 1836.
59. *Waterford Mirror*, 25 May 1836.
60. Major B. Woodward to Drummond, 1 June 1836, N.A., C.S.O.R.P., 1557/1836.
61. Interesting Particulars, *Waterford Chronicle*, 31 March 1838. See S. Jones to Drummond, 25 May 1836, N.A., C.S.O.R.P., 1557/1836. Also, *Tipperary Constitution*, 27 May 1836.
62. Jones to Drummond, ibid.; *Waterford Chronicle*, 31 May 1836.
63. N.A., C.S.O.R.P., 2174/1836.

64. Interesting Particulars, *Waterford Chronicle*, 31 March 1838.
65. Crossley to Drummond, 19 July 1836, N.A., C.S.O.R.P., 2096/1836.
66. Interesting Particulars, *Waterford Chronicle*, 31 March 1838.
67. Drummond to P. Smith, 4 August 1837, N.A., C.R.F., C2/1838.
68. Smith to Drummond, 14 August 1837, N.A., C.S.O.R.P., 1557/1836.
69. Croker to Drummond, 17 August 1837, ibid.
70. *Waterford Chronicle*, 15 September 1836.
71. Villiers Stuart to Crossley, 22 October 1837, N.A., O.P., 29/106/1837.
72. *Waterford Mail*, 16 July 1836.
73. Power, another watchman, in his evidence before the Waterford County Gaol Inquiry, claimed to have been offered £30 by J. Connery a fortnight before the escape. N.A., C.S.O.R.P., 1557/1836.
74. Drummond, 15 August 1836, N.A., C.S.O.R.P., 1557/1836.
75. N.A., O.P., 29/55/1836 & 29/77/1836.
76. Evidence of Thomas Drummond, p. 13.
77. Ibid., p. 16.
78. *Crime in Ireland: Minutes of Evidence taken before the Select Committee of the House of Lords appointed to inquire into the State of Ireland since the year 1835; in respect to Crime and Outrage, which have rendered Life and Property insecure in that part of the Empire*, pt. 1 486, H.L. 1839, XI, I, p. 1251.
79. Croker to Miller, 19 August 1836, N.A. , O.P., 29/60/1836.
80. Evidence of Thomas Drummond, p. 150.
81. *Waterford Chronicle*, 11 April 1837.
82. Ibid., 4 November 1834.
83. Ibid., 13 October 1836.
84. Ibid., 2 August 1836.
85. A.B. *Waterford Mail*, 2 November 1836.
86. *Waterford Mail*, 17 May 1837.
87. *Waterford Chronicle*, 18 May 1837
88. The arrest was based on a description of J. Connery in the *Hue and Cry* on 11 June and 12 November 1836 which had been inserted by the government. Chief Constable Trench to Drummond, 14 April & Drummond, 17 April 1837, N.A., O.P., 31/27/1837.
89. G. Wright to Croker, 19 September 1837, N.A., C.S.O.R.P., 1557/1836; *Waterford Mail*, 23 September 1837.
90. E. Ashbury to Croker, 24 September 1837, ibid.
91. Miller, 16 December 1837, ibid.
92. Crossley to Col. Shaw Kennedy, Inspector General of Constabulary, 23 October 1837, N.A., O.P., 29/106/1837. Crossley was now acting Sub-Inspector.
93. Ibid.
94. Crossley to Shaw Kennedy, 13 January 1838, N.A., O.P., 29/10/1838; John Hearne, Information, 24 April 1838, C.S.O.R.P., 1557/1836. This may refer to James Collins and two others who were convicted of assaulting the police at Villierstown, on 5 June 1837, the night of the fair of Dromana. Two sub-constables went to close the public house when they were attacked by a mob. In the melee one policeman stabbed a man in the thigh with his bayonet. N.A., O.P., 29/60/1837.
95. Crossley to Shaw Kennedy, 13 January 1838, N.A., O.P. 29/10/1838.
96. Ibid.
97. Ibid.
98. Ashbury to Shaw Kennedy, 23 January 1838, N.A., C.S.O.R.P., 1557/1836.
99. Drummond, 26 January 1838, ibid. The reward is a mystery, Drummond, 28 September 1837, ibid., authorised its payment and Miller (p. 46) stated Dillon had received this

sum.
100. Wright to Croker, 22 September 1837, ibid., was sanguine about Dillon's motives, 'I beg to state that I consider Dillon fairly entitled to the Reward, although perhaps activated by Revenge in giving the information'.
101. A Constant Reader, *Waterford Chronicle*, 12 April 1838, states J. Connery drew his knife but put it away when he saw resistance was useless. As there is no mention of a weapon in the police reports this is most unlikely.
102. *Tipperary Free Press*, 31 March 1838.
103. Interesting Particulars, *Waterford Chronicle*, 31 March 1838.
104. Ibid.
105. *Waterford Mirror*, 31 March 1838.
106. T. Ryan to Drummond, 27 April 1838, 29 April 1838, 28 May 1838, N.A., C.R.F., C2/1838.
107. J. Fitzgerald, Memorials, 15 April 1838, 29 April 1838, 28 May 1838, N.A., C.S.O.R.P., 1557/1836.
108. *Waterford Mirror*, 21 July 1838.
109. Acting Constable H. Burke, Information, N.A., C.S.O.R.P., 1557/1836; *Waterford Mail*, 21 July 1838.
110. *Waterford Chronicle*, 19 July 1838; *Waterford Mirror*, 21 July 1838.
111. *Waterford Chronicle*, 19 July 1838.
112. *Waterford Mirror*, 21 July 1838.
113. *Waterford Chronicle*, 23 July 1838.
114. See above, p.1.
115. *Dublin Evening Post*, 29 March 1838
116. See above, p. 27.
117. W.M. Thackeray, *Irish Sketchbook 1842* (London, 1843), p. 51.
118. *Waterford Chronicle*, 23 July 1838.
119. Ibid., 25 August 1838.
120. Carrickshock, Co. Kilkenny the site in 1831 of an infamous episode in the Tithe War in which 12 policemen were killed when the peasantry tried to attack Butler, a process server.
121. *Waterford Mail*, 19 September 1838.
122. Ibid. It seems most unlikely that the Connerys would tell Ryan about their own plot. In *Waterford Mirror*, 15 September 1838, Ryan states that the plot 'had been proved on investigation'. It may be that there is a misprint in the quotation and that it should read, 'one of the convicts' instead of one of the Connerys.
123. *Waterford Mail*, 19 September 1838; *Waterford Mirror*, 15 September 1838.
124. *Waterford Mail*, 19 September 1838.
125. Ibid., 12 September 1838.
126. *Waterford Chronicle*, 20 September 1838.
127. P. Ó Cadhla, *Eachtradh Eibhlís i dTír na nIongantas* (Dublin, 1922), p. 122.

Chapter 5
1. Na Conairigh, (Áine Bean Uí Choinghealla), Seanchas Sliabh gCua, p. 182.
2. L.M. Cullen, *The Emergence of Modern Ireland, 1660-1900* (London, 1981), pp. 18-9.
3. Traditional Waterford rhyme (D. Kiely).
4. Seanchas Sliabh gCua, p. 181.
5. Ibid., p. 182.
6. Tóibín, op. cit., p. 29.
7. Ibid., pp. 30-1.

8. Ibid.; Na Conairigh (Áine Bean Uí Choinghealla).

9. See Chapter one note three above.

10. 'Na Conaries' (Seán Mhic Gearailt), in M. Ó Haodha (ed), 'Seanchas ós na Deisibh' in *Béaloideas*, vol. XIV, 1944 (1945), p. 101.

11. Interesting Particulars, *Waterford Chronicle*, 31 March 1838.

12. Mr. & Mrs. S.C. Hall, *Ireland Its Scenery Character Etc* (London, 1841), vol. I, p. 304.

13. Hanley and Gar (Connors) were two of the great Caravat and Shanavest leaders. Roberts, op. cit.

14. J. O'Donovan to Captain Larcom, 7 July 1841, in J. O'Donovan, Letters containing information relative to the antiquities of the County of Waterford, N.L.I. (typescript), 1928, p. 187.

15. G. Cornewall Lewis, *On Local Disturbances in Ireland and on the Irish Church Question* (London, 1836), p. 227.

16. *Waterford Mirror*, 5 March 1834.

17. Ibid., 8 March 1834.

18. Richard Power, brother of William (p. 118) identified the cause of Poleen/Gow hostility as a vendetta lost in time. 'Witness could not tell the original cause of the quarrel between the parties. He called himself a Gow because his father and grandfather were Gows and for no other reason'.

19. De Tocqueville, op. cit., p. 119.

20. Sylvanus Jones R.M., in his evidence before the Select Committee on Crime 1839, gave an interesting answer in this regard when asked whether he detected any traces of Ribbonism in County Waterford: 'never; I do not think such a System exists; certainly it did not exist during my time. I have never heard that such a system existed in the County since the Time of the Disturbances of the Caravats and Shanvests, many Years ago'. *Crime in Ireland: Evidence, pt. 111, 486, H.L. 1839, XI, I, p. 1254.*

21. Beames, *Peasants and Power*, p. 71.

22. G. Broeker, *Rural Disorder and Police Reform in Ireland 1812-36* (London, 1970), p. 15.

23. Alastair, who is Young Colkitto in Sir Walter Scott's *A Legend of Montrose*, commanded Irish forces in Scotland 1644-7. He died at the Battle of Knocknanuss in 1647, Governor of Clonmel and Lieutenant General of the Catholic Confederate army of Munster. D. Stevenson, *Alastair Mac Colla and the Highland Problem in the Seventeenth Century* (Edinburgh, 1980); D. Ó h-Ógáin, *The Hero in Irish Folk History* (Dublin, New York, 1985), pp. 170-4.

24. James Graham, Marquis of Montrose, as Commander of Royalist forces in Scotland was a Protestant attempting to restore Charles I to his throne. In contrast Alastair 'fought for his family and clan; for his Catholic religion; and for the Highland and Irish Gaelic world against Lowland and English supremacy'. Stevenson, op. cit., dustcover.

25. Ó Cadhla, op. cit., p. 122.

Chapter 6

1. P. Breathnach, *Ár gCeól Féinig* (Dublin 1920), p. 145.

2. *Clonmel Herald*, 19 August 1835.

3. *Cork Merchantile Chronicle*, 12 August 1835.

4. *Lloyds' Register 1833 Shipowners;* C. Bateson, *The Convict Ships* (Glasgow, 1985), 3rd edition, pp. 352-3.

5. *Sydney Herald*, 17 December 1835.

6. *Account of the Expense of the Convict Department, Cork 535, H.C. 1835, XLV, II, p. 8.*

7. Account of Money paid to Surgeon Donoghue of the Ship *Hive* for the use of Convicts

on board that vessel, A.O.N.S.W., 2/8263, p. 81.

8. Statement of Thomas Nutting, 23 August 1835, ibid., p. 73.

9. *Cork Constitution*, 27 August 1835; *Sydney Herald*, 27 December 1835; Loss of the *Hive*, M.L., MS AH 45.

10. Journal of A. Donoghue, P.R.O., Adm., 101/34/9.

11. Ibid.; Printed Indent 1835, *Hive* (2), A.O.N.S.W., X637, pp. 198-9; Irish Indent, *Hive* (2), ibid., 4/7077.

12. Report of Facts connected with the wreck of the Convict Ship *Hive*, Governor's Dispatches, M.L., MS A 1267, p. 1654 [hereafter *Hive* Facts].

13. Ibid., pp. 1649-50.

14. Ibid., pp. 1646-9.

15. Ibid., pp. 1649-50.

16. Loss of the *Hive*, op. cit.

17. *Hive* Facts, p. 1654.

18. A. Berry to A. McLeay, Colonial Secretary, 14 December 1835, A.O.N.S.W., C.S.I.L., 10071/1835 in 4/2282.2; Donoghue to McLeay, 11 January 1836, ibid., 303/1836 in 4/2321.1; Certificate of Sir R. Bourke, 12 March 1836 A.O.N.S.W., 4/4531, p. 190.

19. Loss of the *Hive*, op. cit.; *Hive* Facts, p. 1652; Printed Indent, op. cit., pp. 196-7.

20. Bateson, op. cit., pp. 248-52.

21. Donoghue to McLeay, 14 December 1835, A.O.N.S.W., C.S.I.L., 10071/1835 in 4/2282.2.

22. Berry to McLeay, 14 December 1835, ibid..; Certificate of Bourke, 8 March 1836, A.O.N.S.W., 4/4531, p. 186; J. Arrowsmith, *The London Atlas*, (London, 1835), p. 36.

23. *The Australian*, 18 December 1835.

24. *Hive* Facts, p. 1652; Loss of the *Hive*, op. cit.; R.C. McCrea to McLeay, 23 January 1836, A.N.O.S.W., C.S.I.L., 739/1836.

25. Berry to McLeay, 11 December 1835, A.N.O.S.W., C.S.I.L., 10071/1835 in 4/2282.2.

26. *Sydney Herald*, 14 December 1835.

27. Berry to McLeay, 14 December 1835, op. cit.

28. Ibid.

29. *Sydney Gazette* and *New South Wales Advertiser*, 17 December 1835.

30. Ibid., 22 December 1835

31. Ibid., 12 January 1836.

32. Journal of A. Donoughue, op. cit.; Printed Indent, op. cit., pp. 200-1; Irish Indent *Hive* (2), op. cit.

33. *Sydney Gazette* and *New South Wales Advertiser*, 26 January 1836.

34. *Hive* Facts, p. 1645.

35.Nutting to McLeay, 14 March 1836, A.O.N.S.W., C.S.I.L., 2378/1836 in 4/2322.4.

36. *Hive* Facts, p. 1656; Lord Glenelg to Bourke, 30 November 1836, M.L., MS A 1274, pp. 391-3.

Chapter 7

1. A. Grassby and M. Hill, *Six Australian Battlefields* (North Ryde, N.S.W., 1988), pp. 38-45, 70-103, 134-68.

2. R. Hughes, *The Fatal Shore* (London, 1988), pp. 17-18.

3. A.G.L. Shaw, *The Story of Australia* (London, 1975), pp. 58-60.

4. P.O'Farrell, *The Irish in Australia*, (Kensington, N.S.W., 1987), p. 39.

5. Grassby and Hill, op. cit., pp. 104-33.

6. O'Farrell, op. cit., pp 10-13, has argued that up to very recently the Irish, and more particularly the Catholic Gaelic Irish, have been the dynamic factor in Australian history.

7. J. Waldersee, *Catholic Society in New South Wales 1788-1860* (Sydney, 1974), pp. x, 95.
8. Waldersee, ibid., p. x.
9. A famous put down used in a speech by the radical Dan Deniehy in 1853. The word is Aboriginal and refers to a legendary fabulous monster.
10. Hughes, op. cit., p. 335.
11. O'Farrell, op. cit., p. 29.
12. See above Chapter one, note 19.
13. That contribution is measured in S. Nicholas (ed.), *Convict Workers Reinterpreting Australia's Past* (Cambridge, 1988).
14. *New South Wales Government Gazette*, 27 January 1836.
15. Raby Station Correspondence and Accounts 1832-1836, M.L., MS A 146.
16. M.L., Document 2390, Document 2706.
17. A.D.B., vol. 2, pp. 379-81.
18. Ibid., pp. 381-2.
19. *Sydney Herald*, 15 September 1836.
20. A.D.B., op. cit., p. 381.
21. W.E. Riley Papers, M.L., MS A 111, pp. 203-5.
22. W.E. Riley to H. Dutton, 4 December 1832, Raby Station, op. cit.; Riley Papers, M.L., MS A 106, pp. 109-10; *Sydney Herald*, 13 July 1840.
23. W.E. Riley, The Corobberie, M.L., MS A 109.
24. Raby Station, op. cit.
25. See Dr. Lockyer Potter, 'Cavan' in *J.R.A.H.S.*, vol. XXVI, pt. II, (1940), pp 188-96.
26. *Sydney Herald*, 15 March 1838.
27. See statement of W. Kilpatrick, Superintendent at Cavan, 1 September 1837, A.O.N.S.W., 8604/1837 in 4/2507.2.
28. Waldersee, op. cit., p. 159.
29. A.D.B., vol. 2, pp. 292-3.
30. *Sydney Herald,* 26 September 1836; *The Australian,* Yass Races, 1 November 1836.
31. M. E. Yeo Papers, M.L., MS Q 991.8/Y, Random Notes, p. 11 and Mr. J. Collison's Reminescences No. 5.
32. J. Norton to H. Brooks, 20 June 1838, M.L., MS An 2/1.
33. See A.R. Riley, A.O.N.S.W., C.S.I.L. (Land), 2/7958.
34. S.A. Donaldson to S. Donaldson Sr., 10 July 1838, M.L., MS A 728.
35. See above p. 43-4.
36. Hughes, op. cit., pp. 491-8.
37. Waldersee, op. cit., p. x.
38. Recollections of an Australian Squatter's Wife, M.L., MS A 2105, Draft A, p. 1.
39. S.A. Donaldson to C. O'Brien, 4 July 1838, M.L., MS A 728.
40. *The Australian,* 11 September 1838, 21 September 1838.
41. O'Farrell, op. cit., p. 105.
42. Waldersee, op. cit., p. 259.

Chapter 8
1. Kilmainham Convict Register 1838, N.A., Prisons, 1/10/30.
2. Convict Ships Musters and Other Papers, A.O.N.S.W., 2/8258, p. 33.
3. *Lloyds Register of Shipping,* 1840.
4. Journal of A. Osborne, P.R.O., Adm., 101/24/10; Bateson, op. cit.
5. *Sydney Gazette* and *New South Wales Advertiser,* 8 January 1839.
6. J. and P. Connery to Governor Sir C. A. FitzRoy, January 1850, A.O.N.S.W., C.S.I.L., 221/1850 in 4/2883.

7. Report of the Special Committee (Water) of Sydney City Council, A.O.N.S.W., C.A., 2/8151, p. 5.

8. Tóibín, op. cit., pp. 33-4.

9. F. Clune, *Ben Hall and His Gang (Wild Colonial Boys* 1948) (London, 1975).

10. Grassby and Hill, op. cit., pp. 42-5.

11. Potter, op. cit., p. 195; A.D.B., vol. 2, pp. 123-4.

12. S.A. Donaldson to E. Deas Thomson, 8 April 1841, A.O.N.S.W., C.S.I.L., index entry only could be traced.

13. A.D.B., vol. 2, p. 293.

14. Shaw, op. cit., p. 93.

15. *Guide to Convict Records in the Archives Office of New South Wales* (Sydney, 1981), p. 21.

16. A.O.N.S.W., Assisted Immigrants Inward to Sydney, 4/4840.

17. Ibid., 4/4780, pp. 378-9.

18. St. Mary's Baptisimal Register 1837-43.

19. There is nothing in the Registers of convict applications to marry 1838-50, A.O.N.S.W., 4/4513 and 4/4514 nor in Consents of the Governor and Declarations for Presbyterian Marriages 1826-60, 5/7691.

20. St. Mary's Catholic Burial Register 1841.

21. N. Abjorsen, 'Why we have Canada Bay', *Sydney Morning Herald,* 2 July 1988.

22. M. Kelly, *Paddock full of houses: Paddington 1840-1890* (Paddington, N.S.W., 1978), p. 19.

23. J. M. Ward, *James Macarthur Colonial Conservative 1798-1867* (Sydney, 1981), p. 121.

24. J. and P. Connery to Lieutenant-Colonel G. Barney, 17 March 1843, A.O.N.S.W., C.S.I.L., 2043/1843 in 4/2618.2.

25. Ibid., together with 813/1843 and 2683/1843.

26. *New South Wales Government Gazette,* 22 March 1844; Ticket of Leave Butts, A.O.N.S.W., 886/1844 in 4/4187.

27. *Guide to Convict Records,* p. 115.

28. *The Australian,* 13 April 1841.

29. *Sydney Morning Herald,* 1 February 1843.

30. W.N. Grey to Deas Thomson, 19 November 1842, A.O.N.S.W., C.S.I.L., 8748/1842 in 4/2586.6.

31. Butts of Ticket of Leave Passports, A.O.N.S.W., 568/1848 in 4/4270.

32. *New South Wales Government Gazette* , 9 August 1844; Tickets of Leave Butts, A.O.N.W.S., 2041/1844 (Pat) and 2042/1844 (John) in 4/4192.

33. J. Long Innes to the Principal Superintendent of Convicts, 1 July 1844, A.O.N.S.W., 4/5721.

Chapter 9

1. In 1850 John and Patrick state they have resided at the Swamp for the last 11 years. See P. and J. Connery to Deas Thomson, 6 February and 28 February 1850, A.O.N.S.W., C.S.I.L., 1682/1850 and 2479/1850 in 4/2883.

2. A.R. Riley, op. cit.

3. S.A. Donaldson to Rev. J.W. Donaldson, 6 April 1845, M.L., MS Ad 65/10.

4. Shaw, op. cit., pp. 84-6.

5. Those who died were James Donohue of Cappoquin and Sub Constable James Owens from Dundalk, County Louth. John Lennon, 26, a labourer from Cappoquin, died at Spike Island Prison in 1852. The weavers Thomas, 29, and James, 18, Ryan brothers from Cappoquin had pleaded guilty and only served 2 of their 14 year terms. On 17

May 1851 to Bermuda on board the *Bride* from Kingstown went John Donohoe, labourer from Cappoquin, 25, sentenced to 14 years; Luke Lennon, nailer from Cappoquin, 30, brother of John, 14 years; Mathew Joy, spinner from Carrickbeg, 28, 14 years; and James Crotty, labourer from Cappoquin, 24, 14 years. On 13 Sepember 1850 to Van Diemen's Land on board the *Hyderabad* from Queenstown (Cove) went James Casey, weaver from Clonmel, 30, 14 years; Thomas Wall, sawyer from Cappoquin, 24, 14 years; James Lyons, farmer from Cappoquin, 23, 14 years; John Walsh, farmer from Tourin, nephew of Fr. Spratt, P.P., and brother of Fr. Walsh curate at Cappoquin, 23, 7 years. His transported employees were, Edward Tobin, labourer from Araglin, County Cork, 29, 7 years; Thomas Donovan, labourer from Lismore, 24, 7 years and Richard Brien, labourer from Tourin, 27, 7 years.

6. See R. Davis, *William Smith O'Brien Ireland – 1848 – Tasmania* (Dublin, 1989).

7. Pitt St. Marriage Register 1848, Ferguson Memorial Library, Sydney.

8. A.D.B., vol. 4, p. 224; A. Gilchrist, *John Dunmore Lang* (Melbourne, 1951), vol. 1, pp. 222, 328; C.A. White, *The Challenge of the Years, A History of the Presbyterian Church of Australia in the State of New South Wales* (Sydney, 1951), p. 7; *The Presbyterian*, 10 July 1886; J. Cameron, *Centenary History of the Presbyterian Church in New South Wales* (Sydney, 1905), vol. 1, pp. 13, 34, 44, 82, vol. 2, p. 349; D. S. Myles, *One Hundred Years: Fullerton Memorial Church and Congregation 1838-1938* (Sydney, 1939); *Sydney Morning Herald*, 12 July, 19 July and 22 July 1851. The Free Church was created out of the Disruption of the Church of Scotland in 1843 by those who held ministers could only be appointed by their congregations.

9. J. Fullerton, 'Lecture IV', in *Presbyterian Church New South Wales Lectures on the Sabbath* (Sydney, 1841), pp. 14-5.

10. J. Fullerton, *Ten Lectures with Historical Notices Illustrative of the Anti-Scriptural Nature and Pernicious Tendency of the Doctrines of Puseyism* (Sydney, 1844), preface.

11. Conditional Pardons, A.O.N.S.W., 62/1849 and 63/1849 in 4/4463; *New South Wales Government Gazette*, 6 February 1849.

12. See above p. 82.

13. There was an earlier station called Templestowe whose squatting licence was held by Templer & Cayley. G.J. Macdonald, Commissioner for Crown Lands visited it from 23 to 24 February 1841. It is presumed the proprietors went broke or else sold out to Donaldson. See Description of Runs in New England, c. 1850, A.O.N.S.W., 4/6913; G. Donaldson to S.A. Donaldson, 12 November 1834, M.L., MS A 726; N. Crawford, *Tenterfield* (Tenterfield, 1949), p. 2.

14. A.D.B., vol. 4, pp. 84-6.

15. Crawford, op. cit., p. 3.

16. See Tenterfield Bench Book, 18 November 1847 – 13 June 1856, A.O.N.S.W., 7/73.

17. Copies of Conditional Pardons, A.O.N.S.W., 600/1850 in 4/4472; *New South Wales Government Gazette*, 27 September 1850.

Chapter 10

1. Memorial of J. and P. Connery to FitzRoy, January 1850, A.O.N.S.W., C.S.I.L., 221/1850 in 4/2883.

2. P. & J. Connery to Deas Thomson, 6 February 1850, ibid., 1682/1850 in 4/2883.

3. J. & P. Connery to Deas Thomson, 28 February 1850, ibid., 2479/1850; Billyard to Deas Thomson, 30 March 1850 (annotations), ibid., 3423/1850 both in 4/2883.

4. J. Connery to Deas Thomson, 7 June 1850, ibid., 5500/1850 in 4/2916.

5. O'Farrell, op. cit., pp. 29-34. He argues that the conformity of Dwyer and other transported leaders of the United Irishmen was crucial for Irish Australia. 'The long-

term effects of 1798 was to protect Australia from subsequent Irish nationalism, to dampen their local fires'.

6. J. Connery to Deas Thomson, 24 September 1850, A.O.N.S.W., C.S.I.L., 9038/1850 in 4/2916.
7. A.D.B., vol. 5, pp. 419-20.
8. Ellen became the registered owner in 1885. See Certificate of Title, New South Wales, vol. 768, folio 133, appn 5807, Sydney Land Registry.
9. In J. Connery to Deas Thomson, 3 October 1850 & 24 September 1850, A.O.N.S.W., C.S.I.L., 9417 and 9038/1850 in 4/2916.
10. Pearce to Deas Thomson, 4 October 1850, ibid., 9406/1850 in 4/2916.
11. See Reclamation and Enclosure of Sandhill Sydney, A.O.N.S.W., C.A., 2/647.
12. H.M. Suttor, 'Early Gold Discoveries', *J.R.A.H.S.*, vol. viii, pt. vi, (1922), pp. 317-33. A.D.B., vol. 4, pp. 346-7.
13. *Bathurst Free Press and Mining Journal*, 10 May 1851.
14. 'News from the Interior', *Sydney Morning Herald*, 6 June 1851.
15. *Sydney Morning Herald*, 28 May 1851.
16. Coroner's Inquest, ibid., 8 July 1851.
17. Ibid.
18. Suttor, op. cit., p. 327.
19. *Sydney Morning Herald*, 5 July 1851; Catholic Burials N.S.W. 1851, vol. 368, no. 118,
20. Register of Coroners Inquests, 1848-52, A.O.N.S.W., 4/6612.

Chapter 11

1. See A.O.N.S.W., C.S.I.L., 2316, 2661 and 1869/1852 in 4/3075.
2. P. Connery to FitzRoy, 16 October 1854, ibid., 9019/1654 in 4/3252.
3. FitzRoy, 28 October 1854, ibid., on 9330/1854 in 4/3252.
4. Pearce to Deas Thomson, 24 October 1854, No. 3.
5. W. Elyard to Pearce, 5 January 1855, A.O.N.S.W., 4/3662, p. 10.
6. W. Fitzpatrick to Colonial Secretary, 25 March 1857, ibid., C.A., 2/647.
7. Police Convict Branch Register of Correspondence Received, ibid., 816/1855 in 4/4556.
8. Waldersee, op. cit., p. 251.
9. Registry of Deaths N.S.W. 1857; *Sydney Morning Herald*, 10 September 1857.
10. A.O.N.S.W., C.A., 2/586.
11. P. Connery & J. Hanrahan, Land Titles Office Sydney, vol. 624, no. 528, 1859.
12. Register of Marriages N.S.W. 1866; Register of Deaths N.S.W. 1924.
13. Register of Marriages N.S.W. 1875; Register of Deaths N.S.W. 1919.
14. K. Amos, *The Fenians in Australia 1865-1880* (Kensington, N.S.W., 1988), p. 52. His chapter, pp. 45-77, on Henry James O'Farrell is excellent.
15. O'Farrell, op. cit., p. 215.
16. Amos, op. cit., p. 76.
17. N.S.W. Electoral Rolls, Canterbury, 1869-70 to 1877-8.
18. K. McMenomy in his *Ned Kelly, The Authentic Illustrated Story* (Melbourne, 1984), p. 11, has him working as a woodranger but doubts are cast on this in local research presented by Bob Reece in his provocative 'Ned Kelly and the Irish Connection – a Re-appraisal' in *Tipperary Historical Journal* (1990), pp. 47-62. The John Kelly debate seems set to become as controversial as that of Ned.
19. Ned Kelly A Letter from Jerilderie in Bill Wannan (ed), *The Wearing of the Green: The Lore, Literature, Legend, and Balladry of the Irish in Australia* (Melbourne, 1965), p. 197.
20. O'Farrell, op. cit., p. 137.

21. J. Molony, *Ned Kelly* (Ringwood, Victoria, 1989), pp. 87-8. Originally published as *I am Ned Kelly*. Molony's is an excellent study particularly in its use of folklore.
22. McMenomy, op. cit., p. 91.
23. Wannan, op. cit., p. 189. Edward Kelly's *Jerilderie Letter* was never published in his lifetime but it was used by the Crown at his trial.
24. *Burkes Colonial Gentry,* vols. 1 and 2, (Baltimore, [reprint], 1970), pp. 154-5; A.B.D., vol. 5, pp. 364-6. He remained in charge until 17 June 1879. He was elected for Clare in 1877 but because he did not resign the seat, like his father at Dungarvan, when he was appointed Attorney General, a Committee of Elections of the House of Commons declared the seat vacant on 24 April 1879.
25. Register of Deaths N.S.W. 1880; Burial Records 1880, Catholic Section, Rookwood Cemetery.

Chapter 12
1. Con Costello puts the Irish total at 45,000 in his *Botany Bay* (Cork, 1987), p. 9. The grand total is put at close to 160,000 comprising over 78,000 to New South Wales, over 65,000 to Van Diemen's Land and close to 10,000 to Western Australia in J.C.R. Camn and J. McQuiston (eds), *Australians: A Historical Atlas* (Sydney, 1987), p. 200.

Bibliography

PRIMARY SOURCES

I. Manuscripts
Archives Office New South Wales
Convict Records: X 637 (printed indent); 2/8263 (Convicts' money, *Hive*); 4/4187 & 4/4192 (Ticket of Leave Butts); 4/4270 (Ticket of Leave Passport Butts); 4/4463 & 4/4472 (Conditional Pardons); 4/4513 & 4/4514 (Applications to Marry); 4/7077 (Irish Indent); 4/4556 (Police Convict Branch).
Colonial Architect: 2/586; 2/647.
Colonial Secretary: 1. In-Letters: 100071/1835; 303, 739, 2378/1836; 8604/1837; Index 1841: 8748/1842; 813, 2043, 2683/1843; 221, 1682, 2479, 3423, 5500, 9038, 9406, 9417/1850; 9019, 9330/1854.
2. Immigration: 4/4780; 4/4840.
3. Justice: 4/5721 (Hyde Park Bench); 4/6612 (Coronors' Inquests); 5/7691 (Presbyterian Marriages); 7/73 (Tenterfield Bench).
4. Miscellaneous: 2/7958 (Land); 2/8151 (Water); 4/6913 (Description of Runs).

Genealogical Office, Dublin
Pedigree of O'Conry of Dungarvan, Co. Waterford and Seville, Spain, c. 1650-1780 (MS 164).

Ferguson Memorial Library, Sydney
Pitt Street Presbyterian Church, Marriage Register 1848.

Mitchell Library, Sydney
Donaldson Papers: MSS A 728; Ad 65/10.
The *Hive*: MSS A 1267; 1274; AH 45.
Recollections of an Australian Squatter's Wife: MS A 2105.
Riley Papers: MSS A 106, 109, 111, 146; An 2/1; Documents 2706, 2390.
Mary E. Yeo Papers: MS Q 991.8/Y.

National Library of Ireland, Dublin
Bolton MS 16350: Letters of William Bishop of Waterford and Lismore with supporting testimony from clergy, 14 February 1787.

National Archives, Dublin
1. Chief Secretrary's Office Registered Papers: MSS 2723/1831; 5297, 5643,

5961, 6424/1833; 856/1834; 1323, 2643, 2743/1835; 120, 1332, 1557, 2096/1836.
2. Convict Reference Papers: Patrick and John Connery, C 2/1838.
3. Outrages Papers: M 47, 64, 109, 1831; 1936/1832; 266, 330, 766/1833; 529/1834; 29/28, 29, 34, 56, 61/1835; 29/1/8, 1/9, 14, 20, 55, 60, 77, 78, 85/1836; 29/32, 39, 51, 60, 86, 106/1837; 31/27/1837; 29/10, 65/1838.
4. Kilmainham Convict Register 1838, MS 1/10/30.
5. Tithe Applotment Books: MSS 29/27 1827; 29/23 1829; 29/68 1830; 29/29 1831; 29/9 29/21 29/22 1834.

Public Records Office, London
Journal of A. Donoghue, MS Adm., 101/34/9.
Journal of A. Osborne, MS Adm., 101/24/10.

Rockwood Catholic Cemetery, N.S.W.
Burial Register 1880.

Saint Mary's Cathedral, Sydney
Baptismal Register 1837-43.
Burial Register 1841.

Sydney Land Registry
MSS 624/528/1859; Certificate of Title, 766/103/5807.

University College Dublin
Department of Irish Folklore: Béaloideas (Irish Folklore Commission), Labhrás Ó Cadhla Collection 1936 (MS 109).

II Contemporary Publications
1. Parliamentary Papers (in chronological order).
Account of the Expense of the Convict Department, Cork, [535], H.C. 1835, XLV, II.
Poor Inquiry: Appendix (F) containing baronial examinations relative to con-acre, quarter of score ground, small tenantry, consolidation of farms and dislodged tenantry, emigration, landlord and tenant, nature and state of agriculture; [38], H.C. 1836, XXXIII, I.
Crime in Ireland: Minutes of Evidence taken before the Select Committee of the House of Lords appointed to inquire into The State of Ireland since the year 1835, in respect of Crime and Outrage, which have rendered Life and Property insecure in that part of the Empire, pt. 1 486, H.L. 1839, XI, I.
Census of Ireland 1841; [504], H.C. 1843, XXIV, I.

Devon Commission: Minutes of Evidence taken before her Majesty's Commissioners of Inquiry into the State of Law and Practice in Respect to the Occupation of Land in Ireland, pt. 111 [657], H.C. 1845, XXI, I.

2. Newspapers
Australian, Sydney, 1835-6, 1838, 1841.
Bathurst Free Press and Mining Journal, 1851.
Clonmel Advertiser, 1834.
Clonmel Herald, 1836.
Cork Constitution, 1835.
Cork Merchantile Chronicle, 1835.
Dublin Evening Post, 1838.
Dublin Gazette, 1835-7.
Freeman's Journal, Sydney, 1866.
Limerick Chronicle 1839
National Police Gazette, New York.
New South Wales Government Gazette, Sydney, 1836, 1844, 1849-50.
Sydney Gazette and New South Wales Advertiser, 1835-6, 1839.
Sydney Herald, 1835-6, 1838, 1840.
Sydney Morning Herald, 1843, 1851, 1857.
Presbyterian, Sydney, 1886.
Tipperary Constitution, Clonmel, 1836-7.
Tipperary Free Press, Clonmel, 1836, 1838.
Waterford Chronicle, 1830-8.
Waterford Mail, 1826-39.
Waterford Mirror, 1826-39.

3. Other Contemporary Publications
Arrowsmith J., *The London Atlas* (London, 1835).
De Beaumont, G., *Ireland; Social, Political and Religious* ed. W.C. Taylor, 2 vols. (London, 1839).
Drummond, T., *Evidence of Thomas Drummond, Esq., before the Select Committee of the House of Lords on the State of Ireland in respect of Crime* (Dublin, 1838).
Fullerton, J., 'Lecture IV' in *Presbyterian Church New South Wales Lectures on the Sabbath,* (Sydney, 1841).
————, *Ten Lectures with Historical Notices illustrative of the Anti-Scriptural nature and Pernicious Tendency of the Doctrines of Puseyism,* (Sydney, 1844).
Hall, Mr. and Mrs. S.C., *Ireland Its Scenery, Character Etc.,* 3 vols., (London, 1841-3).
Inglis, H.D., *A Journey throughout Ireland, during Spring, Summer, and Autumn 1834,* 2 vols., (London, 1835).

Lewis, G. Cornewall, *On Local Disturbances in Ireland and on the Irish Church Question* (London, 1836).

Lloyds Register 1833 Shipowners.

Lloyds Register of Shipping 1840.

Madden, D.D., *Ireland and its Rulers since 1829*, 3 parts, (London, 1844).

Ryland, R.H., *The History, Topography and Antiquities of the County and City of Waterford* (London, 1824).

Smith, C., *The Ancient and present State of the County and City of Waterford* (Dublin, 1746).

Thackeray, W.M., *The Irish Sketchbook* (London, 1842).

III Later Works

1. Newspapers
Waterford News, 1937.

Sydney Morning Herald, 1988.

2. Later Publications
Abjorsen, N., 'Why we have Canada Bay', in *Sydney Morning Herald*, 2 July 1988.

Amos, K., *The Fenians in Australia 1865-1880* (Kensington, N.S.W., 1988).

Australian Dictionary of Biography, 5 vols. (Melbourne, 1966-74).

Australians, An Historical Atlas, (Sydney, 1987).

Bateson, C., *The Convict Ships*, 3rd ed., (Glasgow, 1985).

Beames, M.R., 'Rural conflict in Pre-Famine Ireland: Peasant Assassination in Tipperary 1837-1847' in *Past and Present*, no. 81, (1978), pp. 75-91.

————, *Peasants and Power: The Whiteboy Movement and Their Control in Pre-Famine Ireland*,(Brighton, 1983).

Boyle, P., *The Irish College in Paris, A.D. 1578-1901* (London, 1901).

Breathnach, P., *Ár gCeól Féinig* (Dublin, 1920).

Broeker, G., *Rural Disorder and Police Reform in Ireland 1812-1836*, (London, 1970).

Burke, W.P., *A History of Clonmel*, (Waterford, 1907).

Burkes Colonial Gentry, 2 vols., (reprint Baltimore, U.S.A., 1970).

Burtchaell, J., '19th Century Society in County Waterford' in *Decies*, no. XXX, (Autumn, 1985), pp. 25-34.

————, 'A Typology of Settlement and Society in County Waterford c. 1850' in Nolan, W., and Power, T. P., eds., *Waterford History & Society* (Dublin, 1992), pp. 541-78.

Cameron, J., *Centenary History of the Presbyterian Church in New South Wales* (Sydney, 1905).

Clarke, S., *Social Origins of the Irish Land War* (Princeton, 1979).

Clarke, S., and J.S. Donnelly, Jr., eds., *Irish Peasants Violence and Political Unrest 1780-1914*, (Manchester, 1983).

Clune, F., *Ben Hall and His Gang* (*Wild Colonial Boys,* 1948), (London, 1975).

Costello, C., *Botany Bay The Story of the Convicts transported from Ireland to Australia 1791-1853* (Cork, 1987).

Crawford, N, *Tenterfield* (Tenterfield, 1949).

Cullen, L.M., *The Emergence of Modern Ireland 1600-1900* (London, 1981).

Curtis, R., *History of the Royal Irish Constabulary* (Dublin, 1869).

Davis, R., *William Smith O'Brien Ireland - 1848 - Tasmania* (Dublin, 1989).

De Noraidh, L., *Ceol ón Mumháin* (Dublin, 1965).

De Tocqueville, A., *Journeys to England and Ireland*, ed. J.P. Mayer, trans. by L. and K.P. Mayer (New Haven, 1958).

Donnelly, J.S., Jr., *The Land and People of Nineteenth Century Cork; The Rural Economy and the Land Question* (London, 1975).

——————, 'The Whiteboy Movement, 1761-65' in *Irish Historical Studies*, 21, no. 81, (1978), pp. 20-54.

——————, 'The Rightboy Movement, 1785-8' in *Studia Hibernica*, nos. 17-18 (March, 1978), pp. 120-202.

Fitzpatrick, T., *Waterford during the Civil War 1641-53* (Waterford, 1912).

Gilchrist, A., *John Dunmore Lang*, 2 vols. (Melbourne, 1951).

Graham, A.H., 'The Lichfield House Compact 1835' in *Irish Historical Studies*, no. 47 (1961), pp. 209-25.

Grassby, A., and M. Hill, *Six Australian Battlefields* (North Ryde, N.S.W., 1988).

Guide to Convict Records in the Archives Office of New South Wales, 2nd ed (Sydney, 1981).

Hughes, R., *The Fatal Shore* (London, 1988).

Hurst, J.W., 'Disturbed Tipperary: 1830-1860' in *Eire Ireland*, vol. IX, no. 3, 1974, pp. 44-59.

Keeper of Public Records in Ireland, Reports, 11th, 1879; 12th, 1880; 17th, 1885.

Kelly, M., P*addock full of houses: Paddington 1840-1890* (Paddington, N.S.W., 1978).

Kiely, M. B., and Nolan, W., 'Politics, Land and Rural Conflict in County Waterford c. 1830-1845' in Nolan, W., and Power, T. P., eds., *Waterford History & Society* (Dublin, 1992), pp. 459-94.

Lee, J., 'The Ribbonmen' in Williams, T.D., ed., *Secret Societies in Ireland*, pp 26-35.

McCartney, D., 'Electoral Politics in Waterford in the early 19th Century' in *Decies*, no. XX (May 1982), pp. 39-50.

McCurtain, M., 'Prefamine Peasantry in Ireland. Definition and Theme' in *Irish University Review*, IV, (1977), pp. 188-98.

McDowell, R.,B., *The Irish Administration, 1801-1914* (London, 1964).

McMenomy, M., *Ned Kelly The Authentic Illustrated Story* (Melbourne, 1984).

Murray, S., 'Caravats and Shanavests. Factions in Waterford 1805-15' in *Decies*, no. IV, 1977, pp. 9-12.

Myles, D., *One Hundred Years: Fullerton Memorial Church and Congregation 1838-1938* (Sydney, 1939).

Molony, J., *Ned Kelly (I am Ned Kelly,* 1980) (Ringwood, Vic., 1989).

Nicholas, S., ed., *Convict Workers Reinterpreting Australia's past* (Cambridge, 1988).

Nickolls, K., 'The Geraldines of Decies' in *Decies*, no. VII, (January, 1978), pp. 22-3.

Ní Annagáin, M., and S. De Chlainndiolúin, eds., ' *"Londubh an Chairn" Being Songs of the Irish Gael in staff and sol-fa with English Metrical Translations* (London, 1927).

Nolan, W., and Power, T. P., *Waterford History & Society* (Dublin, 1992).

O'Brien, R.B., *Coercion or Redress, A Chapter from the Melbourne Administration, With A Sketch of the Political Career of Thomas Drummond* (Manchester, 1881).

————, *Thomas Drummond Under-Secretary in Ireland 1834-40 Life and Letters* (London, 1889).

Ó Cadhla, P., *Eachtradh Eibhlís i dTír na nIongantas* (Dublin, 1922).

Ó Caoimh, S., 'Na Connairí' in *An Sguab* (June, 1925), pp. 376-7.

O'Donnell, P., *The Irish Faction Fighters of the 19th Century* (Dublin, 1975).

O'Donoghue, P., 'Causes of Opposition to Tithes 1800-1838' in S*tudia Hibernica* no. 5, (1965), pp. 7-28.

————, 'Opposition to Tithe Payments in 1830-31' in *Studia Hibernica*, no. 6, (1966), pp. 69-98.

————, 'Opposition to Tithe Payments in 1832-33' in *Studia Hibernica*, no. 12, (1972), pp. 7-108.

O'Donovan, J., *Letters containing information relative to the Antiquities of the County Waterford*, N.L.I. (typescript, 1928).

O'Farrell, P., *The Irish in Australia* (Kensington, N.S.W., 1987).

O'Ferrall, F., *Catholic Emancipation. Daniel O'Connell and the Birth of Irish Democracy 1820-1830* (Dublin, 1985).

Ó Flannghaile, T., ed., *Eachtra Ghiolla an Amaráin or the Adventures of a Luckless Fellow and other poems by Donnchadh Ruadh Mac Conmara with life of the Poet by the late John Fleming* (Dublin, 1897).

Ó Haodha, M., ed., 'Seanchas ós na Déisibh' in *Béaloideas*, vol. XIV, 1944(1945), pp. 53-112.

O'Hart, J., *The Irish and the Anglo-Irish Landed Gentry when Cromwell came to Ireland; or a supplement to Irish pedigrees* (Dublin, 1884)

Ó Milléadha, P., ed., 'Seanchas Sliabh gCua' in *Béaloideas*, vol. VI, 1936, pp. 169-256.

Ó Muireadhaigh, S., 'Na Carabhait agus na Sean Bheisteanna' in *Galvia*, vol. VIII, 1961, pp. 4-20.

Ó h-Ógáin, D., *The Hero in Irish Folk History* (Dublin, 1985).

Ó Tuathaigh, G,, *Ireland Before the Famine, 1798-1848* (Dublin, 1972).

Ó Tuathaigh, M.A.G., *Thomas Drummond and the Government of Ireland 1835-41*, O'Donnell Lecture, N.U.I., no, 21, 1977.

Pender, S., ed., *Census of Ireland, 1659: A Census of Ireland circa. 1659 with supplementary material from the Poll Money Ordinances (1660-1661)* (Dublin, 1942).

Potter, L., 'Cavan' in *J.R.A.H.S.*, vol. XXVI, pt. II, (1940).

Power, P., *The Place Names of Decies* (London, 1907).

————, *A Compendious History of the United Dioceses of Waterford and Lismore* (Cork, 1937).

Reece, B., 'Ned Kelly and the Irish Connection – a Re-appraisal' in *Tipperary Historical Journal*, (1990).

Roberts, P.E.W., 'Caravats and Shanavests: Whiteboyism and Faction Fighting in East Munster, 1802-1811' in Clarke and Donnelly, eds., *Irish Peasants Violence and Political Unrest 1780-1914*, pp. 64-101.

Simmington, R.C., T*he Civil Survey A.D. 1654-1656 County of Waterford, vol. VI, with Appendices* (Dublin, 1942).

Shaw, A.G.L., *The Story of Australia* (London, 1975).

Stevenson, D., *Alastair Mac Colla and the Highland Problem in the Seventeenth Century* (Edinburgh, 1980).

Suttor, H. M., 'Early Gold Discoveries' in *J.R.A.H.S.*, vol. XXXV, pt. VI, 1922, pp. 317-33.

Swords, L., History of the Irish College Paris, 1578-1800. Calendar of the Papers of the Irish College' in *Archivium Hibernicum*, vol. XXXV, (1980).

Thompson, E.P., 'The Moral Economy of the English Crowd in the Eighteenth Century' in *Past and Present*, no. 50, (February 1971), pp. 76-136.

Tóibín, N., *Duanaire Déiseach* (Dublin, 1978).

Waldersee, J., *Catholic Society in New South Wales 1788-1860* (Sydney, 1974).

Wall, M., 'The Whiteboys' in Williams, T.D., ed., *Secret Societies in Ireland*, pp. 13-25.

Walton, J.C., 'The Subsidy Roll of County Waterford, 1662' in *Analecta Hibernica*, no. 30, (1982), pp. 47-96.

Wannan, B., ed., T*he Wearing of the Green. The Lore, Literature, Legend and Balladry of the Irish in Australia* (Melbourne, 1965).

Ward, J.M., *James Macarthur Colonial Conservative 1798-1867* (Sydney, 1981).

White, C.A., *The Challenge of the Years; A History of the Presbyterian*

Church in the State of New South Wales (Sydney, 1951).

White, J.G., *Historical and Topographical Notes Etc. on Buttevant, Castletownroche, Doneraile, Mallow and Places in their Vicinity*, vol. IV (Cork, 1925).

Williams, T.D., ed., *Secret Societies in Ireland* (Dublin, 1973).

Woodham-Smith, C., *The Great Hunger, Ireland 1845-1849* (London, 1987).

SECONDARY SOURCES

Brynn, E., *Crown and Castle British Rule in Ireland 1800-1830* (Dublin, 1978).

Colmcille, An t-Athair, 'Where was Sliabh gCua' in *Decies*, No. 46, Autumn 1992, pp. 5-9.

Crowley, J., *Jimmy Crowley's Irish Song Book With Music and Guitar Chords* (Cork, 1986).

De Bhaldraithe, T., 'Na Connerys Céirbh Iad?' in *Comhar*, (February 1985), pp. 20-23.

—————, 'Na Connerys' in *The Irish-Australian Connection An Caidreamh Gael-Austraileach*, Grimes, S., and Ó Tuathaigh, G., eds (Galway, 1989).

Mac Giolla Choille, B., 'Na Connerys sa Bhaile' in *Comhar* (April, 1985), pp. 20-21.

Macintyre, A.D., *Daniel O'Connell and the Irish Party 1830-1847* (London, 1965).

MacCartney, D., ed., *The World of Daniel O'Connell* (Cork, 1980).

Mokyr, J., *Why Ireland Starved A Quantitive and Analytical History of the Irish Economy*, 1800-1850 (London, 1985).

Nowlan, K.B., and M.R. O'Connell, eds., *Daniel O'Connell Portrait of a Radical* (Belfast, 1984).

Ó Grada, D., 'Na Connerys' in *Comhar* (March, 1985), pp. 22-5.

Ó Grada, D.F., 'The Connerys: Heroic Villains?', in *Decies*, no. XXXII (Summer,1986), pp.12-5.

Ó Concheanainn, T., *Nua Dhuanaire Cuid III* (Dublin, l978).

Ó Murchu, L., *Na Connerys dramá trí ghníomh* (Dublin, 1974).

Reece, B., 'The Connerys' in *Exiles from Erin; Convict Lives in Ireland and Australia*, B. Reece, ed., (Dublin, 1991).

UNPUBLISHED WORKS

Kiely, M. B., The Connerys Land, Factions and Agrarian Violence in Waterford 1830-38, M.A. thesis, University College Cork, 1987.

INDEX

Capless, John, 39
Cappagh, 1, 34
Cappoquin, 5, 10, 28, 38, 57, 79, 84
Caravats, 9-10, 17, 60-2, 100
Carrickbeg, 32
Carrick-on-Suir, 3, 9-10, 13, 15, 18, 31, 34, 61
Carrickshock, 52
Carroll, Chief Con., 31, 33, 35-7, 56
Casey, James, 32
Casey, John, 32, 39
Castle Hill, 69-70, 98
Cavan, County, 71
Cavan Run, 83
Cavan Station, 72-5, 77, 79, 82-3, 86
Centennial Park, 103
Central Railway Station, 103
Charles II, 5
China, 79
Christmas, William, 44
Clachan, 3
Clare, County, 13, 28
Clashmore, 28, 39, 61
Cleary, John, 52
Clifton Station, 86
Clogheen, 25-6, 37, 44, 56, 60
Cloncoskeran, 7
Clonkerdin, 29
Clonmel, 3, 16, 25, 37, 52, 65
Clontarf, 98
Cockatoo Island, 72
Colligan, 3, 6-7, 13
Colligan River, 3, 33
Collinses, the, 46
Comeragh Mountains, 1, 3, 11, 17, 33, 60-3, 72, 97
Commons, House of, 74
Conditional Pardon, 85-6, 96
Connery, Daniel, 5
Connery, James (jr.), 83-4, 92, 97-8, 100-1
Connery, James (mail), 38
Connery, Mary, 85, 92, 97-8, 100
Connery, Padráig Óg, 80
Connery, Patrick (sr.), 6, 39
Connery, William, 33
Connerys' sister, 35, 38-9
Connerys' uncle, 36
Connell, Laurence, 19
Connell, Thomas, 43
Connaught, 61, 65

Connors, Patrick, 36-7
Constant Reader, 59
Coogee Bay, 89
Coolangatta, 67
Coolnasmear, 5
Cork, 9, 31, 38, 44, 52, 65, 67
Coshmore and Coshbride, 4, 17
Cove, 22, 25, 35, 43, 65-6
Croker, Samuel, 28-9, 33-4, 41, 43
Croneen, Denis, 18
Croneens, the, 18
Crossley, Francis, 13-4, 16, 18, 29, 35-6, 39-40, 42-3, 46, 48
Crotty, Michael, 16
Crotty, Laurence, 19
Cullen, Louis, M., 57
Cummins Hotel, 11
Curragh of Kildare, 72
Curreen, Catherine, 13-4, 16
Currency Lads & Lasses, 69
Curry, W.S., 27, 29
Cuthill, Dr., 92
Crystal Palace, 91

Daniel, John, 39
Darlinghurst, 98
Dawson, Alexander, 97
Dawson, family, 4
De Beaumont, Gustave, 16-7, 22-3, 27
Decies, 3-5
De Paor, Éamonn, 23
Derry, 85
Desmond, Michael, 66
De Tocqueville, Alexis, 22, 61
Devines' public house, 28
Devonshire, Duke of, 27
Dillon, Patrick, 45-6, 48
Doherty, Chief Justice, 29, 42
Donoghue, Anthony, 65-7
Donncha Rua, 4
Donaldson, Stuart Alexander, 74-5, 79, 82-3, 86, 89, 96
Donaldson, Stuart (sr.), 74
Dooley, Fr., 29
Dower, Michael, 43
Doyle, Alexander, 52
Dromana, 5, 11, 41, 57
Dromroe, 5
Drummond, Thomas, 26-8, 31, 35-43, 48, 51, 56, 62, 85-6